A Western Horseman Book

LEGENDS

Outstanding Quarter Horse Stallions and Mares

By Diane C. Simmons

With Pat Close

LEGENDS

Published by
The Western Horseman Inc.

3850 North Nevada Ave.
Box 7980
Colorado Springs, CO 80933-7980

Design, Typography, and Production
Western Horseman
Colorado Springs, Colorado

Cover painting
By Orren Mixer

Printing
Publishers Press
Salt Lake City, Utah

ISBN 0-911647-26-0

INTRODUCTION

IN OUR March 1990 issue, we featured a special tribute to the American Quarter Horse Association in honor of its 50th anniversary. In fact, the Orren Mixer painting on the cover of this book appeared on the cover of that issue. Among other articles, in that March issue, we included brief profiles of a number of legendary Quarter Horse stallions. That issue turned out to be a smash hit, which made us realize that lots of horsemen are interested in the stories of the great horses who helped to form the American Quarter Horse breed. That realization led to this book.

We asked free-lance writer Diane Simmons (see her profile on page 166) to do the leg work in gathering information and pictures of the horses to be featured, and to write the articles. We also searched our WH photo files to glean more photos, and borrowed a number from friends.

In the early days of the AQHA, the registration policies were far different than they are now. Believing that many readers would be interested in those initial policies and the changes made over the years, we asked Jim Goodhue to write about their history. No one is more qualified than Jim to do this. He worked for the AQHA for 33 years; the first 11 as head of the performance department and the last 22 as registrar. And he bred and owned Quarter Horses from 1945 until just a few years ago.

Jim also read the articles about each horse to help us make sure the information is as accurate as possible. We are ex-tremely grateful for his assistance. Jim, who retired in 1992, is now living with his wife, Robin, in Corrales, New Mexico.

I would also like to express our appreciation to all of the people who provided us with information and photos. And I would like to give special thanks to the always-helpful staff in the AQHA's records research and microfilm departments, the American Quarter Horse Heritage Center & Museum, and Phil Livingston of Weatherford, Texas. Phil loaned a number of photographs to us, and provided helpful information about many of the horses.

Even though we have researched as carefully as possible the stories about the horses featured, we realize that this book might contain some errors. That's because information about some of the early horses, such as Shue Fly, is vague or contradictory. Nor was the recording of breedings and pedigrees in the old days as thorough and detailed as it could have been. And many of the old-timers who could set the stories straight have passed on.

If anyone does spot any mistakes, we would appreciate hearing from you. We can make corrections in the next printing.

I would also like to mention that it was a tough call to choose which horses should be featured in this book. We actually planned to feature more horses, but space limited us to 26. However, we are already planning *Legends, Volume 2.* So if your favorite old horse is not in this book, he, or she, might be in the next one.

Patricia A. Close, Editor
Western Horseman Inc.

A HISTORY OF
EARLY AQHA REGISTRATION

By Jim Goodhue

BACK IN 1940, when the founders of the American Quarter Horse Association gathered to form a new breed registry (some would say a new breed) and start keeping records of pedigrees, they literally had to start from scratch—and hearsay.

Most of them had known, or heard about, the deeds of some great old horses. They had seen, or heard about, the conformation that seemed to make it possible for those horses to accomplish whatever great deeds they had done. They knew some of the bloodlines that had produced those outstanding individuals and, of course, the bloodlines passed down from them.

So, it was decided that these three factors were the pegs on which they would hang the bridle of the Quarter Horse breed: performance, pedigree, and conformation.

One decision, which probably seemed minor at the time, was also readily accepted by the founding group. This was spelled out in the first set of printed rules as: "All colors are acceptable except those commonly designated as spotted, pinto, appaloosa, and albino."

There was, however, a wide spectrum of opinion as to the type of performance that was the most important and, therefore, which bloodlines and conformation could produce that performance.

The lack of organized events to prove performance ability was a problem, but the largely hearsay reports of matched races, professional rodeo events, and cutting horse contests gave some clues.

In the case of pedigree, at least one side was to trace to those fine old horses whose memory had started this project (AQHA).

To begin, that great horseman Jim Minnick and a few other official representatives of the association visited some ranches and farms known to produce horses who were thought to be within the desirable limits. From these herds, which naturally included the remudas of the founders, they registered the first horses who were to be known officially as American Quarter Horses.

Then, the public was invited to make application to register any horses the owners thought would meet the three-pronged standard. Such applications were to be accompanied by 25 percent of the registration fee. If the horse was accepted, that initial fee was applied to the registration fee, but if the horse was rejected, the fee was forfeited.

Because the founders had financed the operation of the association by buying stock in it, shares of stock also were offered to any interested party. This gave the shareholder a discount on the price of registering a mare, though stallion registration fees were the same for everyone.

Acceptance basically meant a perusal of the bloodlines stated on the application by association officers and then an examination of the horse by an official inspector. A horse could be rejected on either level. The inspection was an attempt to evaluate each horse on the characteristics of basic soundness and action, as well as the elusive "Quarter Horse type." The inspector might even be able to see a demonstration of the horse's performance ability—or at least hear some glowing descriptions.

The "unknown" blood taken into the registry was largely that of western range-bred horses. It was the same blood, therefore, that had been producing rodeo performers, ranch using horses, and an occasional matched runner. It was thought to have come, in part at least, from the range mustangs and other horses tracing back to the stock imported by the Spaniards as they traversed the American Southwest.

The "known" blood included a few crosses of Arabian and Morgan horses, but the overwhelming majority were either Thoroughbreds or descendants of those horses famed as Quarter Horses even without a registry—Traveler, Peter McCue, Steeldust, etc.

The Thoroughbreds often traced quickly back to famous runners in the eastern United States or even to other countries. For the most part, though, the so-called American Thoroughbred bloodlines were the ones that produced the short speed that blended well in the Quarter Horse lines.

Unfortunately, most of the early breeding records were handwritten, and attempts to decipher some of them probably caused some confusion and errors. Also, most of the registration applications were handwritten, which made it difficult (and in some cases, impossible) to get the correct names of the equine ancestors.

In addition, without a breed registry, there was no standardization of names—either in spelling or in exclusiveness. Cardenal and Cardinal were the same horse;

Jim Goodhue is now retired after working for the AQHA for 33 years.

Photo by Terry D. Moore

Beetch's Yellow Jacket and Beach's Yellow Jacket were the same; and so were Rex Beach Jr. and Rex Beach II . . . Billy Sunday and Huyler . . . Little Earl and Old Earl . . . Coke T and Prince . . . as well as Sid and Morriss' Rainy Day. There were several horses known as Rainy Day, and there were at least three stallions named Joe Bailey.

For clarification, the association sometimes had to amplify the names (even in the unregistered ancestors), such as "Nixon's" Joe Bailey and "Old" Joe Bailey (also known as "Weatherford" Joe Bailey). The horse who was sometimes designated as "Gonzales" Joe Bailey is the one now usually meant when the name is given simply as Joe Bailey—because he was the one who was declared a foundation sire and given the registration number 4 under that name. The association has always, of course, attempted to cut down on this confusion by eliminating identical names and even names that sounded alike though spelled differently.

It became apparent that some mistakes would be made even though a reasonable effort was made to halt the problem. It also became evident that punctuation marks were a part of the problem. For instance, if one horse was named King's Way and another was named Kings Way, there would be confusion.

Also, by the mid-1970s, Quarter Horse racing had grown big enough to be reported by *The Daily Racing Form* and the proper identification of horses in the wagering field was even more important. It appeared that the most helpful change, without making major rule changes, was to eliminate all punctuation marks. This was done in the 1976 *Official Handbook*.

Though some honest errors were to be expected, the very earliest printed rules provided penalties for willful misrepresentation on registration applications—age, breeding, or whatever.

The founders also recognized that some horses might get into the registry who were not totally desirable as foundation stock for the breed, so all horses were registered into what was called the Tentative Registry until such time they became eligible to advance to the Permanent Registry. Advancement depended upon production of acceptable foals. At first, a stallion could advance by siring four foals who were accepted and registered in the Tentative Registry, and a mare had to have two of her progeny registered. As numbers in the registry flourished, the number of registered foals required for advancement also was raised.

When a horse advanced from Tentative to Permanent, he (or she) did not receive a different registration number. He was issued a new registration certificate with a capital "P" in front of the old number.

When both parents of a horse in the Tentative Registry advanced, the younger horse could advance without the requirement of registered offspring. A horse who hadn't yet been registered could go directly into the Permanent if both parents were in the Permanent.

So, the AQHA began to grow but grow slowly. An early goal was to make the association pay for its own upkeep, and registration fees (including transfer fees) were the only income. There wasn't enough money in the kitty to pay for organizing and supervising any sort of performance events—either shows or races. Therefore, on February 1, 1945, a group of people primarily interested in short-distance racing formed the American Quarter Racing Association (AQRA). Its purpose was to conduct racing and keep records on the races and horses who competed in recognized races. These horses simply had to be correctly identified in order to get a certificate from this organization and run in AQRA races. Emphasis was on identification for racing purposes and performance.

The AQRA was not affiliated with the AQHA even though some owners were members of both organizations. Some horses listed in the AQRA were also registered in the AQHA, but others had been registered as Thoroughbreds. Others hadn't previously been registered by any organization, but had one parent in either the AQHA or The Jockey Club, the Thoroughbred registry. Many, as the saying goes, were "by Trailer, out of The Reservation."

Among other things, the AQRA set up standards for grading Quarter racing horses. The system, which was loosely based on classification of Greyhounds at dog racing tracks, designated certain times within each of the seven distances recognized at that time (220 yards through 440 yards) as either D, C, B, A, or AA.

If a horse finished a 350-yard race in 17.8 seconds, for instance, he was given a grade of A, no matter how he placed in the race. Then, he was qualified to run in races written specifically for A horses. Such grading was designed to provide close competition in each race—appealing to both horsemen and the general public.

Because A and AA were the faster grades on this scale, the horses who officially received such grades were placed in the Register of Merit (ROM). This was for recognition of superior race horses and was thought to be a means for helping select breeding stock to produce future runners.

In later years, as horses and tracks became faster, an even faster category was added. This was AAA, and then horses who qualified for the Register of Merit had to be AA or AAA.

Some years later, an even faster category was specified and given the name of Top AAA. This came to be designated in the computer era as TAAA, or AAAT.

At an even later date (1969), when tracks no longer were using these grades to any large extent as gauges for writing races for Quarter Horses, and the Register of Merit was used primarily for advertising or to advance a horse within the registry, the letter grade system was dropped, and a speed index rating by number, based on speed within each distance as compared to the track record for that distance, was adopted. At that point, horses with speed ratings of 80 or higher were included in the Register of Merit.

At about the same time that the AQRA was formed, another group of Quarter Horse enthusiasts was becoming restive. They felt that the AQHA founders were keeping for themselves too many of the advantages of the association, and that the rules and policies promoted by the founders were too restrictive as to conformation, bloodlines, markings, ownership of the registry, etc.

In December of 1945, those people formed the National Quarter Horse Breeders Association (NQHBA). It was to be a breed registry that would include all types of horses that the owners felt to be Quarter Horses. This group's registration rules were much less stringent than those of the AQHA.

This meant that monies and energies that would have been devoted to the AQHA were going to be divided among the three registries. Also, there would be bitter competition among the organizations when various states began legalizing pari-mutuel wagering on Quarter Horse races and had to decide which group was to have the official registry for that state's racing.

So, wiser heads prevailed among the stockholders of the AQHA, and a decision

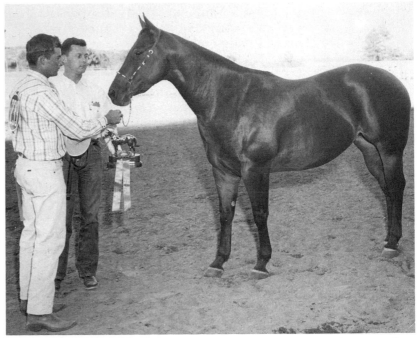

In our WH photo files, we found this picture of Jim Goodhue that was taken at the 1958 Prescott, Ariz., Quarter Horse show. Jim was presenting the trophy for the grand champion to the handler (unidentified) of Sing Song, owned by Helen and Herman Snyder of Pendleton, Oregon. Sing Song was by the Snyders' stallion, Music Mount. At that time, Jim was head of the AQHA performance department. **Photo by Matt Culley**

was made to restructure the association so as to accommodate a wider variety of people interested in the Quarter Horse.

At the election of AQHA officers early in 1946, Albert Mitchell was drafted into the job of president. A noted rancher from New Mexico, he had a national reputation in the livestock field and a clear, unbiased perspective.

Under his direction, the AQHA began making changes in itself as well as overtures to the AQRA and NQHBA about the possibility of a merger. Mitchell hired a full-time executive secretary for the association, Raymond Hollingsworth, who had not been closely aligned to any of the factions that had rigidly restricted the growth of the AQHA. The association was moved to Amarillo, Tex., the home of the new executive secretary, who was charged with handling the daily business operations of the AQHA and with implementing the changes that were to be made. It is said that all of the records of the association fit nicely into three filing cabinets for the move.

An early project was to hire a law firm to reorganize the AQHA into a nonprofit, membership-owned entity, instead of a stockholder-held corporation.

Mitchell was re-elected to the presidency in 1947, and the merger talks continued. When Mitchell felt he had started the AQHA on its turnaround and wanted to step down, his arm was twisted, and he took the job for another year. Work continued toward a merger, and the groundwork was laid for the publication of a magazine, which was needed to help offset the bad publicity and misconceptions the group had attracted.

Mitchell stepped down in 1949, but the reform movement was well under way. The AQHA directors met in Amarillo on July 15, 1949, to study a merger plan prepared by a specially appointed committee. The committee was chaired by race horse man Frank Vessels and included Melville Haskell of the AQRA, as well as other men from diverse areas of the Quarter Horse industry. The plan was approved and then extended to the AQRA and the NQHBA.

On September 30 of that same year, the AQRA voted to accept the merger. After further negotiations and some modification to the original plan, the NQHBA agreed to the merger on November 13.

A major development of the reorganization and merger was the creation of the Appendix listing. It was designed primarily as a means of identifying horses of various bloodlines and giving them an opportunity to compete in shows and races, so as to demonstrate their performance abilities and perhaps help them to advance to the Tentative.

Except for those horses with both parents in the Permanent registry, all new horses were to be listed first in the Appendix until they might qualify for advancement through conformation inspection. Require-

ments for advancement to the Permanent were stiffened by demanding 12 Tentative foals for a stallion and 3 for a mare.

With the exception of registered Thoroughbreds, which had been accepted by both of the newer organizations, all horses listed by the AQRA were to be the equivalent of being in the Appendix or could readily be switched to the Appendix. All horses registered by the NQHBA were to have status equal to the Tentative and could be issued a Tentative certificate simply by paying the fee.

The records of the AQRA and the NQHBA were shipped to Amarillo, and the staff of the AQRA became the racing division of the AQHA. They would continue to promote, supervise, and keep records on Quarter Horse racing. The racing Register of Merit established by the AQRA was officially included in the records of the AQHA.

A few years later, that staff was moved from Tucson to Amarillo, and it became the nucleus of the AQHA performance department. As such, it would continue to maintain records on races and race horses, as well as develop records on working events, such as calf roping and reining. A show Register of Merit was created for all show events under saddle.

Meanwhile, back in early 1950, the old stockholders of the AQHA voted to accept all of the changes being made and, without a dissenting vote, authorized changing the association's charter so as to eliminate stock ownership and to substitute provisions for the AQHA to become a membership-owned organization open to all.

It was not until the printing of the 1989 *Official Handbook* of the association's rules that all references to the NQHBA and the AQRA were dropped from the AQHA rules. By this time, all horses involved and most of the people who had been involved were gone from the scene.

Registrations in the AQHA after the merger grew at an even faster rate. Except for natural differences of opinion, the membership worked together to promote all areas of the Quarter Horse industry. The Appendix listing, however, grew faster than the Permanent and the Tentative combined. So, in 1952, a rule was passed to require a horse to have at least one parent in the Tentative, NQHBA, or Permanent before it could be listed in the Appendix.

That same year, the first eight AQHA Champions were named. This title, which had come about as a part of the merger, specified at that time that any horse in the Permanent, Tentative, NQHBA, or Appendix would be given the title after he/she had earned 20 or more points at approved shows or recognized races, provided that the points had been won in 2 or more shows and 2 or more events, under 2 or more judges, and provided that at least 8 points were won in performance events.

Although there still was some disagreement about the rules of registration, no further changes were made until 1957 when the board of directors voted for a major two-pronged restructuring.

Part one of this plan specified that the studbook of the association would be closed to the use of any horses for breeding other than those already in the registry on December 31, 1961. As of the first day in 1962, the Appendix would be dropped while all horses included in the Permanent, the Tentative, and the NQHBA registries would be lumped together in the one category of complete, full registration. Foals with both parents so listed would be registered directly into the studbook.

Part two of the plan was intended to partially offset problems caused from part one by easing somewhat the requirements for advancement out of the Appendix. The main provision of this section of the plan was that from January 1, 1958, through December 31, 1961, any horse in the Appendix could advance to the Tentative part of the studbook by either passing conformation inspection or qualifying for one of the Registers of Merit. Previously, they had to do both.

Well, faster than one can spell "guerrilla warfare," dissension began growing in the ranks. So, at the 1959 AQHA convention, a compromise was whittled out of the divergent opinions. It basically was a four-parter:

1/ As of January 1, 1962, all horses in the Permanent, Tentative, and NQHBA were to be known as "numbered" Quarter Horses. That was to be the one category of full registration, and there were to be no divisions. No longer would the "P" designation be placed in front of the registration number.

2/ The only outcross would be to registered Thoroughbreds. A foal with one numbered Quarter Horse parent and a registered Thoroughbred parent would go into a listing known as the New Appendix. He could advance only by qualifying for a Register of Merit and passing conformation inspection. He was then a numbered horse with full privileges.

3/ Horses who did not advance out of the New Appendix could compete in races and performance events, but could not be used for breeding registered foals and could not be shown in halter classes. It was meant only to be a springboard into the "numbered" registry through competition.

4/ No more horses were to be added to the old Appendix, although those already in it could perform in events under saddle and still had the right to advance if they earned a Register of Merit and passed conformation inspection—or if both of their parents went into the "numbered" book.

At the 1959 convention, it was also resolved that all bylaws and rules affecting registration would be subject to change only by the board of directors. Since then, the executive committee has no longer had this privilege.

Those changes were followed in 1960 by a convention rule change that allowed mares in the old Appendix to advance to the numbered registry by passing conformation inspection even if their bloodlines did not qualify them for the usual inspection. This rule came to be known as the 60 Special, partly because mare owners had to act fast on the offer.

Also in 1960, to address the fear among some breeders that these new cut-and-dried rules would exclude some superior horses from registration, the board of directors wrote a new rule that came to be known as the Hardship Clause. This authorized the executive committee to declare eligible for registration an animal the majority of the committee considered worthy of registration even though he/she lacked some of the registration rule requirements.

This rule, in turn, raised objections from those who felt that "others" would receive advantageous treatment, and from the executive committee, which could see itself swamped with requests for such action from owners with both valid and not-so-valid cases. So, this rule received revisions at almost regular intervals.

The Hardship Clause disagreements finally were resolved at the 1977 convention with the adoption of a three-part program that would go into effect on January 1, 1978. At that time, 1/ The Hardship Clause pertaining to all problems except white markings was abolished; 2/ The regular registration procedures could be used to register eligible horses up through their 4-year-old year, but horses 5 and older no longer could be registered under any circumstances; and 3/ Horses in the New Appendix could be used for breeding and their foals likewise listed in the New Appendix if the other parent was a numbered Quarter Horse.

Another long-simmering question for the association was the use of artificial insemination. This was handled by making its use legal, but restricting its use to the time and place of collection. The rule, which was accepted at the 1966 convention, also allowed the AQHA to inspect the premises of anyone employing this procedure.

At the 1966 AQHA convention, the title of AQHA Supreme Champion was created. This title was to be reserved for horses who could prove themselves outstanding in three fields: working events, racing, and halter.

In mid-1971, another title was created to recognize excellence. This was the Superior (Event) Horse title, given to any horse earning 50 or more points in one specific event.

White markings, which had been a bone of contention virtually since the first rules were announced in 1940, was addressed by the 1971 convention. For the first time, specific lines marked the limits of allowable white.

This proved to be more restrictive than some owners were willing to accept though, and the so-called Excessive White Hardship Clause was put into effect in 1973. This allowed for registering a horse with a small amount of white beyond the specified lines, if at least one of his parents had proved outstanding in approved events.

A lawsuit in 1976 brought out the fact that the rules of registration pertaining to white markings did not provide sufficient "due process" for owners when their horses were rejected under the rules. After that, the rules specified that the AQHA office would notify each owner whose horse might be denied registration by the white rules that he or she could appear before the AQHA executive committee to state the case for the horse in question.

In 1978, the AQHA board of directors voted to do away with the White Hardship Clause for breeding stock. It would be in use only for geldings and spayed mares after that time.

Beginning January 1, 1993, the amount of allowable white markings was raised. Although the increase was not as much for breeding stock as it was for geldings and spayed mares, the areas of the horse on which allowable white was expanded were areas that had stopped the registration on many stallions and mares with only superficial white over the original lines. For non-breeding animals, the increase was noticeably more.

This summary is by no means a complete history of AQHA registration policies, but it does cover the early rules that helped form the American Quarter Horse as a breed. The stories in this book show what great horses could be bred within those rules.

CONTENTS

Page

12 WIMPY P-1

18 PEPPY

22 KING P-234

31 POCO BUENO

38 POCO TIVIO

45 KING FRITZ

54 THREE BARS (TB)

64 DOC BAR

72 BARBRA B

77 CHICARO BILL

82 QUEENIE

87 JOE HANCOCK

95 COWBOY P-12

100 SHUE FLY

Page

106 HARD TWIST

110 HOLLYWOOD GOLD

114 BERT

117 TOP DECK (TB)

120 GO MAN GO

125 DEPTH CHARGE (TB)

130 PLAUDIT

135 QUICK M SILVER

139 STAR DUSTER

143 JOE REED P-3

149 JOE REED II

155 LEO

166 PROFILE

167 REFERENCES

1 WIMPY P-1

Wimpy was awarded the number 1 in the AQHA registry.

WIMPY ACHIEVED everlasting recognition in the world of Quarter Horses by being awarded the number 1 in the AQHA registry. This sorrel stallion was bred and raised by the King Ranch, Kingsville, Texas.

However, there seems to be uncertainty as to when he was foaled. In his book, *The King Ranch Quarter Horses*, Bob Denhardt gives the foaling date as 1935 in one place, 1936 in another, and 1937 in still another. AQHA Stud Book No. 1 gives Wimpy's foaling date as 1935,

and a King Ranch ad in the No. 2 Stud Book, published in 1943, shows a picture of Wimpy and gives his age as 8, which would indicate he was foaled in '35. Yet, Wimpy's official AQHA record gives his foaling date as 1937, as given on his original registration application.

In terms of Wimpy's contributions to the Quarter Horse industry, it makes no difference when he was foaled. But this discrepancy is mentioned in case Quarter Horse history buffs question it.

When the AQHA was organized, the

Wimpy P-1 as a young horse. Phil Livingston, who provided this photo, says he believes it was taken at Fort Worth just before the halter judging when Wimpy was named grand champion stallion.

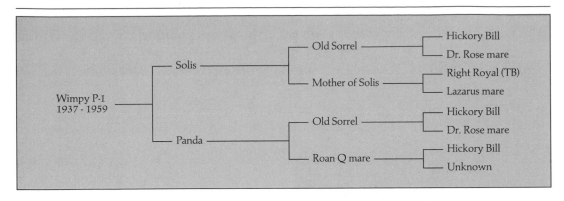

```
                                      ┌─── Hickory Bill
                         ┌── Old Sorrel ───┤
                         │            └─── Dr. Rose mare
              ┌── Solis ──┤
              │          │              ┌─── Right Royal (TB)
              │          └── Mother of Solis ──┤
Wimpy P-1 ────┤                         └─── Lazarus mare
1937 - 1959   │
              │          ┌── Old Sorrel ───┤ Hickory Bill
              │          │            └─── Dr. Rose mare
              └── Panda ──┤
                         │              ┌─── Hickory Bill
                         └── Roan Q mare ──┤
                                      └─── Unknown
```

first directors decided that numbers 2 through 19 in the stud book would be issued to those stallions they considered to be the foundation stock for the breed. The coveted number 1, they agreed, would go to the horse named grand champion stallion at the 1941 Fort Worth Exposition and Fat Stock Show.

This turned out to be a popular idea, and many of the best stallions of that era were led into the ring to be scrutinized by judge Jim Minnick. Most of them were better known than Wimpy. But after Minnick watched all of the horses move, and studied each one closely, he chose Wimpy as the grand champion stallion. The reserve champion: Silvertone, a palomino owned by Lee Underwood of Wichita Falls, Texas.

Wimpy was returned to the King Ranch, where he spent most of his life. A look at his pedigree shows that he was a double-bred Old Sorrel. Old Sorrel, of course, was the foundation stallion of all the King Ranch Quarter Horses.

According to *The King Ranch Quarter Horses*, Old Sorrel's sire, Hickory Bill, was registered in the appendix of The American Stud Book as a Thoroughbred. Denhardt states that Hickory Bill was sired by Peter McCue, and was out of Lucretia M., a bay mare registered with the Jockey Club for racing purposes only.

Raced in Illinois before he was taken to Texas, Hickory Bill was reportedly clocked in some sizzling times for a quarter-mile, half-mile, and five-eighths mile. He evidently had speed to burn.

Halter and Performance Record: None.

Progeny Record:

AQHA Champions: 1	Performance-Point Earners: 4
Foal Crops: 22	Performance Points Earned: 196
Foals Registered: 174	Race Starters: 1
Halter-Point Earners: 13	Superior Halter Awards: 2
Halter Points Earned: 351	Superior Performance Awards: 1
Performance Registers of Merit: 4	

A photograph of Orren Mixer's well-known painting of Wimpy.

Wimpy was a double-bred Old Sorrel.

Wimpy as an older horse.

The Old Sorrel, grandsire of Wimpy and foundation sire of the King Ranch Quarter Horses. He was foaled in 1915, and this picture was taken shortly before his death in 1945. It is said that he was a good-looking horse in his younger days.

He was also a good-looking horse, and started siring some top horses right away. One of them was Old Sorrel, who was out of a mare once owned by a Dr. Rose, a dentist. When she was bred to Hickory Bill, however, she was owned by George Clegg, an outstanding breeder in south Texas.

Not much is known about this mare, although Denhardt states that she was supposed to have been a Thoroughbred. The King Ranch bought her and her suckling colt from Clegg. The colt was never given a formal name. He was simply referred to as the Old Sorrel.

Like all King Ranch stallions, Old Sorrel was used as a ranch horse, and proved to be a superior cow horse. From his second crop of foals came a colt named Solis, who was out of a mare referred to as the mother of Solis. She was a classy Thoroughbred mare—one of many that the King Ranch had acquired from a gentle-

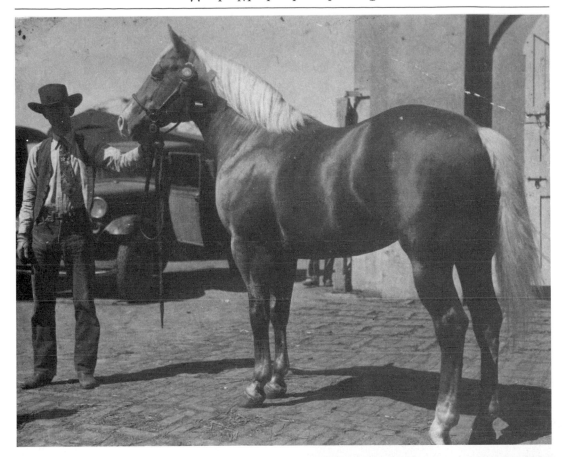

If Wimpy had not placed first at Fort Worth in 1941, this horse—Silvertone— might have earned the number 1 in the AQHA registry. Silvertone placed second to Wimpy.

Photo Courtesy of Phil Livingston

man named Sam Lazarus, according to Denhardt.

Solis was also broke and used as a ranch horse to determine if he was worthy of being used for breeding. He was, and one mare he was bred to was Panda, a daughter of Old Sorrel. Yes, half-brother was bred to half-sister, and the result was Wimpy. Regarding this inbreeding, Denhardt stated the following in his book:

"Breeding half-sisters to half-brothers may seem a little tight—and it does make Wimpy inbred. Inbreeding can be a dangerous procedure for the average breeder working with only 30 or 40 mares and 3 or 4 stallions. It appears, however, that when it is practiced by a master breeder and geneticist such as Bob Kleberg, it works. Careful culling and intelligent and intuitive selection of individuals encourages success, and the desired characteristics are thereby doubled and tripled until they are set.

"Wimpy proved to be a great breeder, and he sired many great sons and daughters. The best were retained by the King Ranch, and their excellence and their reputation is known only locally. Some of his offspring were sold to members of the

Marion's Girl, ridden by Buster Welch, was the NCHA World Champion in 1954 and 1956. She was sired by Silver Wimpy, which made her a granddaughter of Wimpy.
Photo by William C. Mueller

15

Bill Cody, an outstanding son of Wimpy. He sired Joe Cody and a number of other good horses who excelled in halter and performance. The handler shown here is Dr. Darrell Sprott. Foaled in 1944, Bill Cody was the AQHA Honor Roll (high-point) Halter Horse in 1952.

Showdown, one of Wimpy's best sons, won numerous halter championships and sired some great halter horses. Owned by O.G. Hill Jr. of Hereford, Tex., he's shown here at the 1957 Quarter Horse show in Midland, Tex., where he was the reserve champion stallion.

general public, however, and they gained justifiable fame."

Some of Wimpy's better-known offspring included Bill Cody, Little Wimpy, Wimpy II, Silver Wimpy, Showdown, and Red Wimpy. Their influence as sires is still being felt today. Take Bill Cody, the 1952 AQHA Honor Roll Halter Horse, for example. One of his best sons was Joe Cody, an AQHA Champion and a leading sire of reining horses. He was owned by Tom Fuller's Willow Brook Farms, Catasauqua, Pennsylvania. And one of Joe Cody's best sons is Topsail Cody, owned by Bob Loomis, Marietta, Oklahoma. Topsail Cody won the National Reining Horse Futurity in 1980, and has sired many outstanding reiners.

Bill Cody also sired Codalena, who was out of the mare Watt's Niki. A sorrel mare foaled in 1952, Codalena became an outstanding producer, with six AQHA Champions. They were Texas Pine, Pine Pancho, Pine Chock, Pine's Codalena, Pine's Leana, and Barry Pine—all sired by Poco Pine.

Silver Wimpy became a leading maternal grandsire of AQHA Champions.

One of Showdown's greatest daughters was Pandarita Hill, a chestnut foaled in 1954 who was the AQHA Honor Roll Halter Horse in 1959. She's shown here with owner B.A. Skipper Jr. Pandarita Hill was out of the mare Mayflower Daugherty, by Hot Rock.

Photo by James Cathey

However, he is probably best remembered as the sire of Marion's Girl, an outstanding cutting mare in the 1950s—and the NCHA World Champion in 1954 and '56. She was bred by Clarence Scharbauer Jr., and throughout her cutting career she was owned by Marion Flynt of Midland, Tex., and ridden by Buster Welch.

Both Showdown and Wimpy II became leading sires of AQHA Champions. Several of Showdown's AQHA Champions included Caliente Hill, Show Maid, Show Tip, Showdown Wimpy, and Linda Showdown. Wimpy II also became a leading maternal grandsire of AQHA Champions.

Wimpy has no show record with AQHA, and it's possible that he was never shown again after his win in Fort Worth. During his tenure on the King Ranch, he sired about 170 sons and daughters that were registered with the AQHA. Then, when he was 23 years old, the King Ranch gave him to their long-time friend George Clegg, who had bred the Old Sorrel. Later, because of illness, Clegg had to sell the horse, and the buyer was Rex Cauble of Houston. Cauble got just a few foals by Wimpy before this memorable horse died on August 14, 1959.

Gitana Chica, one of Wimpy's good daughters who won a number of halter classes. Foaled in 1956, she was out of La Bandolina, by Tomate Laureles. This photo was taken in 1959.

PEPPY

PEPPY CARVED his niche in the early days of the Quarter Horse industry as a show horse, and then as a sire. Bred by the King Ranch and foaled in 1934, he became the first horse to be extensively shown by the ranch as an example of its breeding program. Later, when he was retired to stud, he sired a number of good horses.

According to some older horsemen, the King Ranch horses in the 1940s, '50s, and '60s were of a definite type. This included both Wimpy and Peppy. They were stout, well muscled, and smooth. They stood about 15 hands, had good heads, withers

to hold a saddle in place, and were usually a sorrel color with a minimum of white. Compared to the old bulldog horses, they showed the Thoroughbred in their breeding without having too much leg or being slim-gutted. The King Ranch horses were bred by men who used horses—and used them hard—and knew what it took to have a sound, functional mount.

Like other breeders of that era, the King Ranch evidently liked a lot of run in the pedigree of even their cow horses. Many old-timers didn't believe in raising anything that couldn't catch a cow pretty darn

Peppy P-212 was a success in both showing and breeding.

Photo Courtesy of Phil Livingston

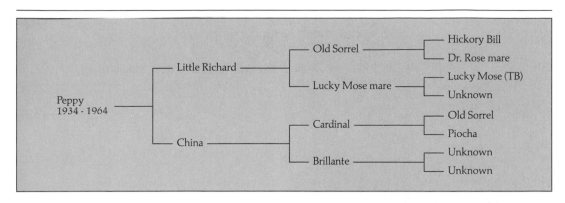

			Hickory Bill
		Old Sorrel	Dr. Rose mare
	Little Richard		Lucky Mose (TB)
		Lucky Mose mare	Unknown
Peppy 1934 - 1964			Old Sorrel
		Cardinal	Piocha
	China		Unknown
		Brillante	Unknown

fast. In fact, Ott Adams, a renowned breeder in the early days, once said, "If they can't run, they should be valued by the pound."

Getting back to Peppy, a look at his pedigree shows that he, like Wimpy, was linebred to Old Sorrel, the foundation sire for the King Ranch breeding program. Peppy's sire, Little Richard, was a son of Old Sorrel and was out of a Lucky Mose (TB) mare. According to Bob Denhardt, in his book *The King Ranch Quarter Horses*, the ranch used Little Richard as a sire from 1927 to 1937. When the AQHA was organized, the ranch registered 18 of Little Richard's fillies, but only one colt: Peppy. Apparently Little Richard's other sons went into the ranch's cow horse remuda.

Peppy's dam, China, was by Cardinal (sometimes spelled Cardenal), another son of Old Sorrel. All of Cardinal's sons were gelded and used as cow horses on the ranch, according to Denhardt. But eight of his daughters were eventually registered. The dam of China was Brillante, thought to be a Thoroughbred.

Peppy stood a hair taller than 15 hands and weighed around 1,200 pounds. He was that beautiful red color typical of King Ranch horses. He was cool, calm, level-headed, and kind. He could run 440 yards in 22 seconds and a handful of change. Like all King Ranch studs of that era, he was also used on the ranch to determine how good a cow horse he was. And he proved that he could handle cutting and roping with equal ease and ability.

Peppy's outstanding conformation and talent didn't escape the sharp eye of Bob Kleberg, who decided the stallion would be the best possible advertising for the King Ranch's breeding program. With that decision made, Peppy was taken on the

Halter and Performance Record: None.

Progeny Record:

Foal Crops: 29	Performance Points Earned: 34
Foals Registered: 193	Performance Registers of Merit: 2
Halter-Point Earners: 11	Race Money Earned: $3,119
Halter Points Earned: 99	Race Registers of Merit: 1
Performance-Point Earners: 5	Race Starters: 2
Leading Race Money Earner: Hot Pepper ($3,119)	

show circuit and, before long, there wasn't a wall big enough, nor a mantel long enough, to hold the ribbons and trophies he collected. The stallion was the first King Ranch representative to receive such broad attention.

The stallion's show career began in 1936 with the Texas Centennial in Dallas. Peppy stayed on the show circuit for 5 years, with most people feeling he was unbeatable. Almost without fail, he was judged grand champion in one competition after another.

All of those shows were held before the AQHA began keeping show records. Consequently, Peppy's wins are not shown on his official record.

At the 1940 Southwestern Exposition and Fat Stock Show in Fort Worth, he was named grand champion Quarter Horse stallion. At this same show the following year, the King Ranch entered Wimpy, not Peppy. Wimpy, of course, won the grand championship—and became number 1 in the AQHA stud book.

Possibly the King Ranch felt Wimpy was the better horse of the two, but many horsemen at the time disagreed. According

Peppy was cool, calm, level-headed, and kind.

Cuero, a 1942 chestnut son of Peppy bred by the King Ranch. This photo was taken at the New Mexico State Fair (date unknown) where Cuero had been named grand champion stallion. From left: Frances Woofer, fair queen; Heber Stewart, Cuero's owner; judge C.M. Botts; and Raymond Hollingsworth, AQHA executive secretary in the late 1940s and '50s.

Photo by James Cathey

Peppy's Pokey, an AQHA Champion son of Peppy, was foaled in 1946, out of the mare Muchacha Colorado. The picture was taken when Peppy's Pokey was named grand champion stallion at the National Western Stock Show in Denver (year unknown). The owner was given as Bob Etter, Holly, Colorado.

to Denhardt, a number of horsemen liked Peppy better because they felt he had a little more quality and refinement. Denhardt also says that George Clegg, who showed many of the King Ranch horses in that era, favored Peppy over Wimpy.

Peppy was last shown at the 1941 Tucson Livestock Show, where he won the title of grand champion cow horse stallion. After that, he began stud duties at the King Ranch.

As Kleberg had hoped, Peppy proved to

be an outstanding sire. Denhardt says that although Peppy is best known for the mares he sired, some of his sons were outstanding as well. One in particular was Peppy's Pepper, foaled in 1944 out of the mare Cubana. The ranch sold him as a yearling to Loyd Jinkens of Fort Worth. In 1946, Jinkens sold him for a reported $26,500, the highest price paid at that time for a Quarter Horse, according to Denhardt. Peppy's Pepper was almost unbeatable in the show ring.

Another Peppy son was Peppy's Pokey, foaled in 1946, and shown extensively in the Midwest. He earned an AQHA Championship, and sired several foals that went on to earn ROMs in the arena.

One of Peppy's daughters was Cacuchia, who, when bred to Wimpy, produced Showdown. Owned by O.G. Hill Jr., Showdown had an outstanding show career and became a leading sire of AQHA Champions.

Because most of Peppy's fillies had talent for cow work, Denhardt says they were put into the King Ranch broodmare bands. But many of his colts were sold because of the demand for them. Several were used in the breeding programs at Washington State University and Michigan State University. And the University of Illinois used horses of Peppy breeding in its program.

For some years, a horse named Pep-Up was registered as a son of Peppy, but after the AQHA received what it thought to be sufficient documentation, it changed the records to show that Pep-Up was a son of Macanudo. According to a knowledgeable source, here is *possibly* what happened:

Back in the early 1940s, the Waggoner Ranch in north Texas bought two young stallion prospects from the King Ranch. One was a son of Macanudo, and the other a son of Peppy, known as Pep-Up. Apparently during shipment—maybe because of rain and mud—the identification of the two horses was switched. The stallion used by the ranch as a sire for many years was thought to be Pep-Up, and his foals were registered accordingly. But somehow it was determined that the stallion was actually the Macanudo son.

This explains the confusion in the pedigree of some "Peppy" horses—even more contemporary horses such as Mr San

Peppy and Peppy San, full brothers by Leo San and out of Peppy Belle. Peppy Belle was originally thought to be by Pep-Up, by Peppy. However, records now state that she was a granddaughter of Macanudo.

When Peppy was 12 years old, the Klebergs loaned him to a friend, Alex Gregg of Birney, Mont., for one breeding season. Then, when Peppy was 19, the Klebergs felt they no longer needed Peppy in their breeding program, and loaned him to Gregg once again. The agreement stipulated that Gregg give the old horse a good home for the rest of his life. By this time, Gregg had moved to a ranch near Sheridan, Wyo., where he handbred the horse. After Gregg died, his widow moved to a small ranch southwest of Sheridan, at Bighorn.

She took Peppy with her. In an article in the October 1966 issue of *The Quarter Horse Journal*, Mrs. Gregg was quoted as saying:

"All of us loved him very dearly. There wasn't a man at the barns who complained about the extra work they were asked to do to take care of Peppy; he had a marvelous, winning personality.

"He was most happy here (the Bighorn ranch); I think even happier than he had been at the Sheridan place.

"He had a nice paddock with plenty of green grass, trees, a blanket when needed, and a nice, warm stall at night with a young filly in the stall next to him.

"The young filly meant a lot to his happiness, as did his carrots; he wouldn't eat until his carrots were placed in his feedbox with other food."

On February 23, 1964, Peppy did not have his usual healthy appetite. Mrs. Gregg and others watched him carefully. Within 48 hours, the vet was called. No one wanted Peppy to suffer, and the vet advised putting down the grand old horse.

He died in Bighorn, on February 24, 1964, at the age of 30. He was buried under the shade of his favorite tree.

Tamet, a grandson of Peppy, was by Tamo and out of the mare Regret. Foaled in 1955. Tamet had a successful show-ring career, and is shown here at the Santa Rosa (Tex.) Roundup (year unknown), where he was named grand champion stallion. **Photo Courtesy of James Cathey**

This granddaughter of Peppy, Little Lou Pep, was by Peppy's Pokey. She was a yearling when this picture was taken at the 1953 Colorado State Fair. She was owned by Everett Willhite, Holly, Colorado.

3 KING P-234

His conformation set the standard for Quarter Horse judging for more than a decade.

VIRTUALLY EVERYONE who came in contact with King "had to have him." Those who owned him touted him as the greatest horse of his time. Those who didn't own him wanted him. Yet no one realized at that time that this horse would become one of the Quarter Horse industry's cornerstones while simultaneously establishing a dynasty.

Bred by Manuel Benavides Volpe of Laredo, Tex., he was foaled June 25, 1932.

His sire was the famous Zantanon, by Little Joe by Traveler. His dam was Jabalina, by the Strait Horse by Yellow Jacket by Little Rondo. There was no such thing as an American Quarter Horse Association when King was foaled, but the stallion's conformation would later set the standard for Quarter Horse judging for more than a decade.

The early '30s were not a time of precise record-keeping, but fortunately, Volpe

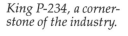
King P-234, a cornerstone of the industry.

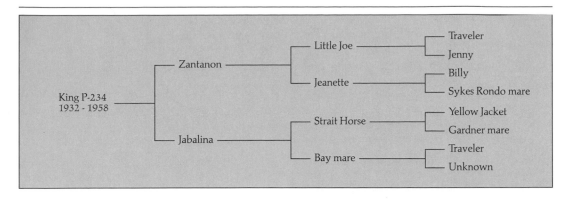

```
                                           ┌─── Traveler
                            ┌─ Little Joe ──┤
                            │               └─── Jenny
               ┌─ Zantanon ─┤
               │            │               ┌─── Billy
               │            └─ Jeanette ─────┤
King P-234 ────┤                            └─── Sykes Rondo mare
1932 - 1958    │
               │                            ┌─── Yellow Jacket
               │            ┌─ Strait Horse ─┤
               │            │               └─── Gardner mare
               └─ Jabalina ─┤
                            │               ┌─── Traveler
                            └─ Bay mare ─────┤
                                            └─── Unknown
```

was a rather meticulous man who kept a small notebook in his possession. He was born in Mexico, but received his education in the United States. As the story goes, his luck with oil made him financially secure. That was fortunate, since he had an eye for fine horses.

It was Volpe's little black book that carried the record of King's foaling. His entry said, "Brown, hogbacked mare (Jabalina) from Binkley, dropped a dark bay horse colt by Zantanon on the 25th of June, 1932."

Zantanon, King's sire, was well-known on both sides of the Mexico/U.S. border. The stallion was hauled back and forth across the Rio Grande. When he was on the Mexican side, he out-distanced almost every taker in match races, even though he was sadly underfed. Reports have also said that in more than one instance, he was treated with harshness bordering on cruelty. Still, he ran. And still, he won because of his fleet-footed courage. He was often referred to as the Man o' War of Mexico.

When Zantanon was 14, Volpe bought him. He handed Eutiquio Flores $500 and the thin, undernourished horse returned to Laredo with Volpe. He eventually recovered his health and began breeding mares. One of them was the hogbacked Jabalina, whose name has often been misspelled as Javalina because the Mexican pronunciation of the letters *b* and *v* are virtually indistinguishable to Anglo ears.

Before going further, Jabalina's story should be told, since it carries its own interesting quirks. Apparently, Jabalina's owner, Fred Binkley of Encinal, Tex., was a gentleman who would place a wager on just about anything. And, apparently,

Volpe was inclined in the same direction. It seems Binkley's wife was pregnant, and Binkley bet Volpe she'd produce a boy. The stakes were Jabalina against one of Volpe's heifers. Well, Mrs. Binkley was delivered of a baby girl and Jabalina changed owners.

According to a story written by Bruce Beckmann in *The Quarter Horse Journal* (August '90), Binkley felt he came out the best in that deal since he once said, "When I started to break that mare, I had to give up on her. She wasn't worth a damn. A man on foot could have outrun her."

After he'd had Jabalina a while, Volpe concurred with Binkley's assessment of the mare's personality. He admitted she was difficult to handle, but all her foals were just the opposite. They were gentle, willing, and easy to work with. The colt who especially fell under this description was foaled June 25, 1932. Named Buttons by

A 1954 photo of Royal King, one of King's best sons, when he stood reserve champion stallion at the Wyoming State Fair. He was owned by Earl Albin, Comanche, Texas. An outstanding cutting horse, Royal King became a leading sire of AQHA Champions.

Photo by James Cathey

There was something about his bearing, his posture, his overall look that James liked.

Volpe, he was sold to a neighbor, Charles Alexander of Laredo, for $150. He was only a month old at the time of the sale, so Volpe kept him until he was weaned.

The next personality entering the Buttons/King story was Byrne James, a professional baseball player from Encinal, Texas. James and his wife were driving down a dusty Laredo street when they spotted the colt. King was just a yearling, a blood bay with mane, tail, and feet dipped in ebony. There was something about his bearing, his posture, his overall look that James liked.

As the story goes, James took one look and knew he "had to have" the colt. King was being led by a Mexican boy, and James figured the only way to find out more was to follow the duo. Everyone eventually wound up at Charlie Alexander's house. The two men began their palaver, and James shelled out $300 (some accounts say $325) to buy the blood bay. He had to have him, and he got him. Although $300 is a meager price today, it was practically a king's ransom in the early '30s.

Both James and his wife became closely attached to the bay. In fact, it was Mrs. James who changed his name from Buttons to King. She thought King was far more appropriate for a horse with such regal bearing. Later, when he acquired the registration number of P-234, horsemen began referring to him as King P-234. Even today, he's known as King P-234, because his number is so easy to remember.

Byrne James liked King so well that he purchased Jabalina, but he didn't have the mare very long because she soon drowned in a stock pond. (Some accounts say James also purchased Zantanon, King's sire, from Volpe for $500.)

James wasn't able to spend a lot of time with King during the spring and summer, since those were the months he played for the New York Giants. The remainder of the year, however, he handled the hundreds of chores on his James Ranch. Many of those tasks were related to cattle, which meant King was put to general ranch work as soon as he was old enough and big enough to carry a saddle and rider.

When King was fully mature, he stood

Jess Hankins and King.

between 14.2 and 15 hands and tipped the scale somewhere between 1,150 and 1,200 pounds. The proud-looking, well-muscled, and beautifully proportioned young stallion was already attracting widespread attention throughout south Texas.

By the time King was a 4-year-old, James was roping calves from him. As often as he could, James took King to the ranch of Winn Dubose, who lived near Uvalde. It was there they did most of their roping. Then, sometime around 1936, James loaned the blood bay stallion to Dubose. No one knew it at the time, but that one act was destined to alter King's future, as well as the future of the entire breed.

Dubose was considered one of the better ropers of the region, and it didn't take him long to advance King far beyond the calf roping basics taught to him by James. The young stallion took to cattle with natural ease, impressing Dubose, who was once quoted by Bob Gray as saying, "He (King) was very quick to learn,

and good-natured for a stallion. He had a lot of cow sense. I wouldn't say he was the fastest horse I ever rode, but there was no lost motion. He was quick out of the box and quick to get to a calf." Dubose had King no more than 3 days before he began taking him to ropings.

Dubose decided he "had to have" the horse, and he did get him after paying James $500. He roped from the young stallion, and began breeding him to outside mares for a $10 stud fee, along with free board for the mares. He once admitted his lack of organized record-keeping, saying no one realized Quarter Horses would ever be registered. And, certainly, no one suspected King would be used as a model for that yet-to-be-established registry.

Around 1936, the Hankins brothers entered the King picture. Jess, Lowell, and J.O. were a rather close-knit trio from the

No one suspected King would be used as a model for that yet-to-be-established registry.

25

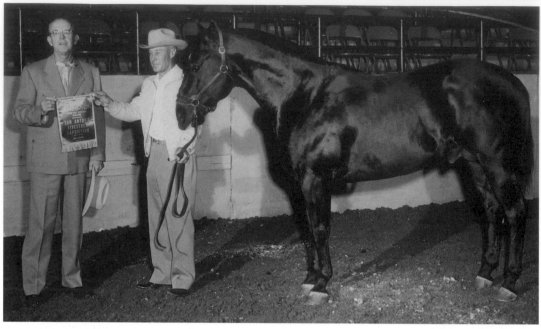

King Glo, 1953 son of King at the 1958 San Antonio Livestock Exposition where he stood grand champion stallion. He was shown by T.C. Stoner and owned by J.O. Hankins. An AQHA Champion, King Glo sired many outstanding offspring.

King's Pistol, an outstanding son of King, with owner-rider Jim Calhoun, Cresson, Texas. An AQHA Champion, King's Pistol was also the 1957 NCHA World Champion Cutting Horse. This photo was taken in 1958 at the Sand Hills Hereford and Quarter Horse Show, Odessa, Texas.

Photo by James Cathey

Rocksprings, Tex., area. They were cattlemen and horsemen, and it wasn't unusual for the three of them to run a combined total of 100 to 150 broodmares on their ranches. The one thing the brothers had in unlimited abundance was an eye for a good horse.

"Jess had a boy by the name of Jack Harris who worked for him for years," related Lowell. "One day, Jack and Jess were out riding. Jess was on a mare he thought a great deal of. The two of them were talking, and Jess told Jack he'd breed that mare if he could find a stallion he thought was better than she was. It so happened Jack had heard about King being at Winn Dubose's place. He told Jess about the stallion, and Jess decided to take a look at him."

It was 75 miles from Jess' ranch to Dubose's. None of the Hankins brothers had ever seen King, but just in case he liked him, Jess gathered up his saddle mare and made the trip. Jess was once quoted in *The Cattleman* magazine as saying, "Before we even stopped the truck, I knew I had found the horse to whom I wanted to breed my mare, and I also knew that someday I was going to own that stallion. I thought then, and still think, he was the most magnificent horse I had ever seen."

Jess Hankins—just like Alexander, James, and Dubose before him—had to have the blood bay stallion.

Dubose didn't particularly want to sell the stallion, whose coat had a curious way of dappling with gold flecks during the

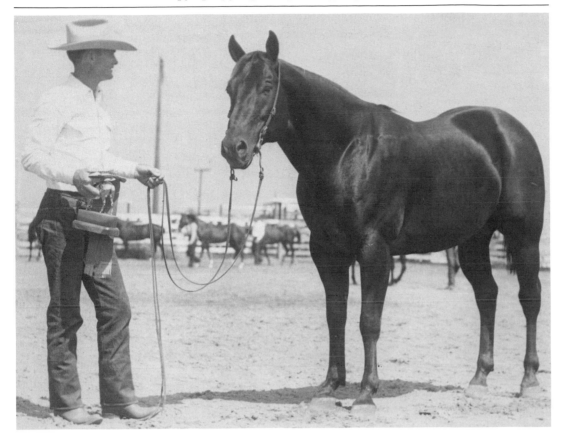

Black Gold King, another AQHA Champion son of King, owned by Raymond Early, Wharton, Texas.

summer months. The two horsemen went back and forth over the situation. Jess kept making offers and Dubose kept refusing. They kept at it for more than a year. Finally, Hankins offered Dubose $800, and Dubose accepted.

At last, Jess had the horse he wanted. But, after all that maneuvering, Jess really didn't have $800! He'd spent his available cash on a load of calves. He turned to brother Lowell for a loan.

"No one but Jess had seen King at the time," said Lowell, "but I can tell you, Jess was set on having him. He came to me and said he needed $800 to buy him. Daddy was worried about the deal, saying $800 was a tremendous amount of money. There were a lot of roping clubs starting up around then, and I figured King must be good if Winn Dubose thought so highly of him. I told Daddy I felt it would be okay, that King would make us some money as a stud horse."

J.O. Hankins can also remember when Jess had to have King. "Jess didn't really have the money," recalled J.O. "He'd spent his cash on some calves. So, he went to Lowell and borrowed to buy the horse.

"That horse literally became a member

Here's a 1958 picture of King Flit taken when his owner, R.Q. Sutherland of the RS Bar Ranch, Kansas City, Mo., presented him, along with four broodmares, to Kansas State College (now university) in Manhattan. Shown with King Flit, who was by King and out of Flit by Leo, are (l-r): Dr. W.R. Stuart, RS Bar veterinarian; John Ballweg, RS Bar manager; and Walter Smith and Rufus Cox of Kansas State.

Easter King, a 1951 son of King in a photo taken at the 1954 Colorado State Fair. The handler is not identified, but the owner is listed as LaRue Gooch of Simla, Colorado. Easter King became best known as the sire of Hollywood Jac 86, the outstanding sire of reining horses, and Easter Gentleman, another good reining horse sire.

**Photo by
Stewart's Photo**

The neighbors couldn't believe that Hankins had actually paid $800 for a horse.

of the Hankins family. He was well-trained with an unbelievable rein. He was a stallion, but always gentle. He also had something no other horse I ever saw before or after him ever had. It was something special. A look. A manner. And his hair. Even if you didn't brush him, his hair still looked like silk. I never saw anything like it."

With money in hand, Jess returned to Dubose. The deal was finalized, but Dubose imposed some stringent conditions before Hankins could actually take possession of the horse. The primary stipulation was that Dubose would keep King until he finished out the roping season on him. The last two contests were scheduled for July 4, 1937. Dubose kept his word and, at 2 a.m. on July 5, 1937, he delivered the bay to Hankins.

It didn't take long for word to spread through Rocksprings about King and Jess Hankins. The neighbors couldn't believe that Hankins had actually paid $800 for a

horse. Didn't he know there was a Depression? No horse could be worth $800, especially not then. It was a fortune in those days.

It was true that the country's economy wasn't in outstanding shape in those days. Dubose had been standing the stallion for $10. Jess upped it to $15 the first season he owned him. It went to $25 the following year. He doubled it the third season, bringing it to $50. Once again, the neighbors were talking. This time, they predicted Jess wouldn't get one mare booked to King. Once again, the neighbors were wrong.

The fourth season, Jess upped the fee to $100 and, according to statements he made years later, he had to turn away 80 mares. Eventually, King's stud fee settled at $500.

By 1940, when the AQHA was established, King was putting progeny on the ground that would make him one of the industry's most famous and respected stallions of all time.

King's first major contribution to the registry was a bay filly out of Queen H, who was by a son of Old Joe Bailey of

Weatherford. It was J.O. Hankins who owned the mare and the filly. J.O., however, didn't count himself fortunate in the ownership since, as he put it, the filly who was foaled in April of 1940 was the "ugliest thing I'd ever seen."

Nelson Nye, in the November 1949 *Quarter Horse Journal*, quoted J.O. as follows:

"When I was on my way over to Jess's place to breed the mare back to King, I stopped a few minutes in town. Several men who saw this foal said it looked to them like such a fine mare should have done better than that. I was ashamed for anyone to see the dang thing and offered then and there to take $75 for her, but nobody wanted her. Later on, when she had filled out a little, you would hardly have known her. In July, I took her to a colt show in Kerrville and she placed first in her class. The following July, I took her to Stamford and, although only a yearling, she was named grand champion mare. I called her Duchess H . . . and she is one of the best matrons of my broodmare band today."

The following year, the ugly duckling was followed by a full sister named Squaw H. This was the mare destined to attract a broad spectrum of attention. Unlike her sister, it wasn't necessary for her to progress from ugly duckling to graceful swan. She was a swan from the beginning—pretty as well as fast. The mare was greased lightning on the track, and she also stood grand champion mare in 1945 at the Tucson Livestock Show. Other names on the racing side of King's siring ability were Hank H and 89er. He later became the double-grandsire of Hanka, the dam of Tonto Bars Hank, a winner of an early All-American Futurity.

Even though King threw speed, he's best known for the tremendous performance ability and cow sense in his offspring. Some years ago, when so much emphasis was being put on Thoroughbred blood and speed in Quarter Horse breeding

Gay Widow, a daughter of King who won at halter and performance, was owned and shown by Julia Reed, Meridian, Texas. When bred to Three Bars (TB), Gay Widow produced Gay Bar King. This photo was taken in 1953 at Plano, Tex., where Gay Widow won the reining and stood grand champion mare. **Photo by James Cathey**

programs, King breeding sort of fell out of favor. But with the growth in cutting, cow horse, and reining events, King's blood became treasured more than ever.

Several of his best sons were Poco Bueno, Royal King, King's Pistol, and Continental King. Another of his sons, Power Command, sired King Fritz, who established his own dynasty of reining and cow horses on the West Coast.

Today, King is remembered like a member of the Hankins family. "He had

When King was bred to Miss Taylor, he sired Cactus King (left) in 1948 and Poco Bueno (right) in 1944. They won the produce of dam class for Miss Taylor at the 1950 Fort Worth Fat Stock Show. Shown (l-r) are Britt Fulps, owner of Cactus King; Jess Hankins, who bred both horses; and Bob Hooper, then president of AQHA.

**Photo by
Skeet Richardson**

the most unbelievable disposition I'd ever seen on a horse," said Lowell, "and he passed it on to his colts and fillies. When he was younger, I think you could have taken two twine strings and had him breed a mare with nothing more than that.

"And he was so athletic. My place was about 2½ miles from Jess's ranch. I used to ride over and get King. I'd ride him back to my ranch to breed my mares and then take him back to Jess when we were finished. Sometimes I couldn't resist having a little fun with him. I'd move the reins just a little and that horse would be gone before I'd finished. He'd make you

uncomfortable he was so fast. I'll tell you . . . I've never known another Quarter Horse like him. He was unique."

King died of a heart attack March 24, 1958. He was 26 years old. He sired 658 registered foals in 23 crops. He had 104 halter-point earners, and 106 working-point earners, and sired 20 AQHA Champions. And even now, years after his death, the industry is still influenced by third-, fourth-, and fifth-generation King-breds.

"I still have horses going back to King," says J.O. Hankins. "We buried him in the trap where he used to run on the ranch in Rocksprings. We still own the ranch."

And, in a way, they still own King . . . the horse so many people just "had to have."

POCO BUENO

BRED BY Jess Hankins of Rocksprings, Tex., Poco Bueno was foaled in 1944. He and his sire, King P-234, were destined to become one of the industry's most famous father/son teams, standing in one-two order on the AQHA leading sires list in the 1950s. In retrospect, it's difficult to tell where the greatness of one stopped and

Poco Bueno and King were destined to become one of the industry's most famous father/son teams.

This is perhaps the most widely recognized photo of Poco Bueno, and was taken by John A. Stryker of Fort Worth.

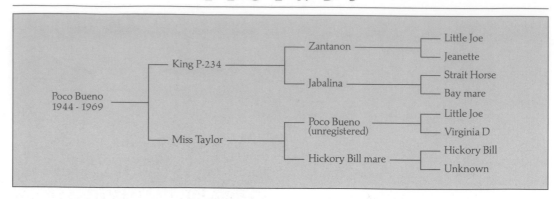

			Little Joe
		Zantanon	Jeanette
	King P-234		Strait Horse
		Jabalina	Bay mare
Poco Bueno 1944 - 1969			Little Joe
		Poco Bueno (unregistered)	Virginia D
	Miss Taylor		Hickory Bill
		Hickory Bill mare	Unknown

Halter and Performance Record: 37 Halter Points; 8 Performance Points; Performance Register of Merit; and AQHA Champion.

Progeny Record:

AQHA Champions: 36	Performance-Point Earners: 118
Foal Crops: 24	Performance Points Earned: 3,617.5
Foals Registered: 405	Performance Registers of Merit: 84
Halter-Point Earners: 163	Superior Halter Awards: 21
Halter Points Earned: 3,522	Superior Performance Awards: 13

Pine Johnson is the man whose name is most closely associated with Poco Bueno.

Photo by James Cathey

the greatness of the other began. Rather than establishing a definitive line of demarcation between themselves, they blended together in a virtually unequaled combination of siring superiority.

As his pedigree shows, Poco Bueno was out of Miss Taylor, a good producer, who was by a horse called Poco Bueno. Because this Poco Bueno was not registered, his grandson out of Miss Taylor could be registered with the same name.

Poco Bueno and King didn't bear a striking physical resemblance to one another. The father was a blood bay while the son was a less glamorous brown (although he was sometimes described as a dark bay). But both had great athletic ability. Put Poco Bueno in a cutting arena and he became a blur of lightning-fast speed. He could cut a rank cow from the herd and make it look oh so easy. He also had the gentleness of his sire.

Jess Hankins had two brothers, Lowell and J.O. Lowell recalls, "We used to hold our own Hankins auction sale in San Angelo, Texas. All we sold was our own stock. I can't guarantee it, but I think ours was the second Quarter Horse sale in Texas.

"Anyway, back then, I had anywhere from 40 to 60 mares. J.O. always kept 30 to 40, and Jess had anywhere from 20 to 30. Based on those numbers, we could usually come up with 60 head or better for our sales.

"Of course, Jess had King then. J.O. had Joe Traveler, who was an own son of Traveler, and I had Diamond Bob who was Champion Quarter Running Horse in '49. Basically, though, all the stallions represented the same type bloodlines.

"We sold Poco Bueno as a long yearling and, even then, we had a pretty good idea of his quality. I can remember the day we loaded the sale horses. We put them on a 40-foot trailer and included King in the bunch. Naturally, we didn't intend to sell him, but people always seemed to get a kick out of seeing him, so we'd bring him along to the sales.

"J.O. climbed up on the sideboards and looked down in the trailer. Poco Bueno happened to be standing right under his eyes. He took a long look at him and then hollered back at Jess, 'Buddy, I think maybe you're making a mistake selling this one.'

"There was a time when I had thoughts about buying Poco Bueno from Jess. He'd already talked with someone else about the colt, but I could have gotten him if I'd really tried. As it was, we took him to the sale."

That sale was the first time Poco Bueno made headlines. He sold for $5,700, which was a rather outrageous price during that particular era—1945. The brown colt was purchased by E. Paul Waggoner, who owned the famed Waggoner Ranch at Vernon, Texas. And that's where the brown horse spent the rest of his life.

His show career got started early, when he was named champion yearling stallion at the Texas Cowboy Reunion Quarter Horse Show in Stamford.

He subsequently stood grand champion stallion at some of the country's leading livestock shows in the '40s: Denver's National Western Stock Show, the Southwestern Exposition and Fat Stock Show in Fort Worth, State Fair of Texas in Dallas, and the American Royal Livestock Show in Kansas City.

As a 4-year-old in 1948, Poco Bueno started his performance career as a cutting horse, and his amazing ability helped him to quickly acquire an impressive record—and a legion of fans.

Although Bob Burton started Poco Bueno under saddle, it was Pine Johnson who primarily showed him in cutting contests. When the brown colt arrived at the Waggoner Ranch, Fagan Miller was the ranch manager. He remembers that "a lot of people rode Poco Bueno in cutting until Pine Johnson went to work for Mr. Waggoner. From then on, it was Poco Bueno and Pine." In fact their names almost became synonymous.

"To tell you the truth," Miller contin-

Poco Bueno was described as solid brown or dark bay. He stood 14.3 and weighed about 1,150 pounds.

At the 1953 Fort Worth Stock Show, Poco Bueno was named grand champion stallion, and also won the get-of-sire class. Shown here are E. Paul Waggoner, with the trophy, and George Tyler. **Photo by Skeet Richardson**

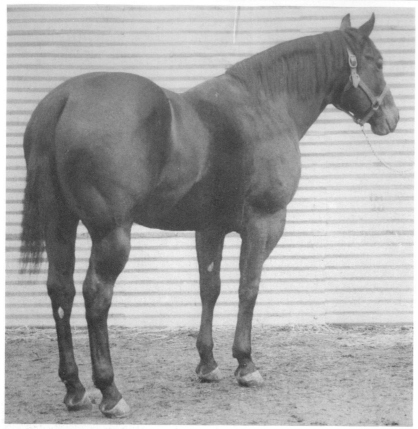

A three-quarter rear shot of Poco Bueno when he stood grand champion stallion at one of the major livestock shows, probably in the late 1940s.
Photo by James Cathey

Poco Dell, one of Poco Bueno's best sons, became an AQHA Champion and a leading sire of AQHA Champions. Foaled in 1950, he was out of Shady Dell, by Pep-Up. He was owned and shown by Jimmie Randals of Montoya, New Mexico. This photo was taken in 1956 at Plainview, Tex., where Poco Dell was named grand champion stallion. **Photo by James Cathey**

ued, "Poco Bueno was the greatest horse I've ever been with, and I've been around a lot of them. He was easy to handle. Gentle. And smart. Nearly all his colts were the same way."

According to Miller, Poco Bueno bordered on the unbelievable in the cutting arena. "That horse could jump backward almost as fast as he could jump forward. It took a real rider to stay with him, and he lost more than one.

"To my way of thinking, it was Poco Bueno who started the cutting horse business. Even after he was old and retired, people came from all over the country just to see him. I still have a lot of horses who trace to him, and I have two grandsons who sire as good a sons as Poco Bueno did. That's what I call greatness that lasts."

Like his sire, however, Poco Bueno's popularity did decline somewhat for a few years when his old-fashioned Quarter Horse type took a back seat to the more Thoroughbred type. But, what goes around comes around—and when horsemen started looking for more working blood, especially cow sense, the popularity of the Poco Buenos soared— and it's still flying high.

In his heyday, the brown stallion was retired from the show ring and cutting pen at an early age because of the mares being booked to him. "He eventually commanded a stud fee of $5,000, which was the highest of any Quarter Horse of that time," wrote Ray Davis (*Western Horseman*, February '70). "He was also the first Quarter Horse to be insured for $100,000. His popularity created a ready market for his foals. Regardless of the mares to whom he was bred, his foals were uniform in appearance and performance ability."

He sired numerous AQHA Champions—such as Poco Bob, Poco Dell, Poco Pine, Poco Lena, Poco Stampede, Poco Tivio, Poco Bow Tie, and Poco Champ, plus many others. A number of his sons went on to become great sires, as well. Of his daughters, the most famous was Poco Lena, foaled in 1949 out of Sheilwin. She became an AQHA Champion and one of the best cutting horse mares of all time. When she was retired for breeding, she produced Doc O'Lena and Dry Doc. Both were sired by Doc Bar, and both

34

Poco Bueno showing the agility and cow savvy for which he and his descendants became famous. Pine Johnson is the rider.

Poco Champ, an AQHA Champion son of Poco Bueno, foaled in 1950. Out of the mare Sheilwin, he was a full brother to Poco Tivio. Poco Champ sired several AQHA Champion sons and daughters, and a number of offspring who earned ROMs in arena events. Poco Champ had just won an open cutting when this picture was taken, but the date and location of the show are unknown.

Poco Lady Pep, a classy daughter of Poco Bueno out of the mare Lady Pep-Up X7, by Pep-Up by Macanudo. Foaled in 1956, she was grand champion mare at Stamford, Tex., where this picture was taken. She was owned by E. Paul Waggoner.

contributed tremendously to the cutting horse industry.

Margaret and Arnold Kontogeorge of Hanceville, Ala., are two more people who remember Poco Bueno. "Arnold and I went to work at Waggoner's in 1966," says Margaret. "All three of us—Arnold, me, and Poco Bueno—were the same age. We were all born in '44. At that time, we didn't know how lucky we were to be

there . . . to be part of Poco Bueno."

By 1966, Poco Bueno was retired and living at the Santa Rosa Roundup grounds. "It was part of the Waggoner Ranch," explained Margaret. "The ranch itself was 500,000 acres, and Santa Rosa had show barns along with polo and rodeo grounds. It was eventually sold to the community

Poco Stampede was another of Poco Bueno's good sons. Out of the mare Pretty Rosalie, he was foaled in 1952, became an AQHA Champion, and sired several AQHA Champions. This photo was taken in Fort Worth in 1955, where he won the AQHA junior cutting. Ridden by Jack Newton, he was owned by G.F. Rhodes of Abilene, Texas. **Photo by James Cathey**

Poco Bueno, at age 20, on the Santa Rosa rodeo grounds, part of the Waggoner Ranch. This photo courtesy of Frank Perkins. **Photo by H.D. Dolcater**

Poco Bueno's best-known daughter was Poco Lena, foaled in 1949 and bred by Waggoner. She was later owned and shown very successfully in cutting by Don Dodge in the 1950s, and then later by B.A. Skipper Jr. (shown here) of Longview, Texas. Skipper, who rode the mare with a seat belt to help him stay aboard, showed the mare to the NCHA Reserve World Championship in 1959, '60, and '61. Later, the mare was bred twice to Doc Bar and produced Doc O'Lena and Dry Doc. This photo was taken at the 1959 NCHA Tournament where Poco Lena tied for first with Poco Mona. Also shown are Byron Matthews and Milo Sullivan, NCHA president and secretary-treasurer, respectively. **Photo by James Cathey**

of Vernon, but the ranch was like an entire city. It even had its own water system."

Poco Bueno was given the run of Santa Rosa. He had his own pasture, but the gates were left open so the old stallion could come and go as he pleased. His stall was a large, round one, with heat lamps in the ceiling. Nothing was spared when it came to his comfort.

"He had arthritis pretty bad by then," continued Margaret, "and walked with most of his weight on his back feet. I can remember Fagan Miller calling him the 'old man.' Arnold and I borrowed a camera so we could take pictures of Poco Bueno. We still have them."

Margaret spent a lot of hours with Poco Bueno while Arnold went about his day's chores. She would sit in the stallion's stall, scratching him behind the ears while he laid his head in her lap. "He was like a big, gentle, affectionate dog," she mused. "I never saw him act like what we think of as a typical stud. He stayed on the ranch until the day he died, and everyone made sure he never suffered."

"Poco Bueno was born April 10, 1944,"

36

At the 1955 Santa Rosa Roundup in Vernon, Tex., one of Poco Bueno's daughters, Poco Maria, sold for $15,000 to Kay Poulan. Shown here are Buster Welch, who took over training of the mare; E. Paul Waggoner; Poco Maria, who was out of Little Red Ant; Kay Poulan; and Fagan Miller, who had started the mare in cutting. Note the three reverse Ds on Waggoner's pants and shirt. This was the brand for Waggoner's Three Ds Stock Farm at Arlington, Tex., part of his overall ranching operation. This was the show place for his horses, and the actual home of Poco Bueno. Waggoner cattle were branded with three reverse Ds, and the horses with one reverse D.

Photo by James Cathey

said Fagan Miller. "He died November 28, 1969. Mr. Waggoner had died 2 years earlier on March 3, 1967. "We knew it was time to let Poco Bueno go when we had to start helping him up. Nobody wanted him to suffer, and Mr. Waggoner had left specific instructions about the horse in his will. He was to be buried in a standing position in a grave across from the ranch entrance on Highway 283. We lowered him into the ground with winches, and then packed dirt around him. That's the way Mr. Waggoner wanted Poco Bueno to be left."

The plot of ground was landscaped with trees and grass. A granite marker, weighing 4 tons, was engraved with his name, picture, and the following: *Champion and Sire of Champions.*

Poco Bueno, like his sire, was special. He may not have been as royal-looking as King, but he commanded deep respect throughout the industry. Notice, if you will, that no one ever referred to the brown stallion by a nickname. He was never Pokey or Bueno. Then, and now, he was Poco Bueno.

Poco Pine, an outstanding son of Poco Bueno, was foaled in 1954 by the mare Pretty Rosalie. He was an AQHA Champion and a leading sire of AQHA Champions, including Dollie Pine, foaled in 1960. When bred to Zippo Pat Bars, Dollie Pine produced Zippo Pine Bar, one of today's leading sires of western pleasure horses. This photo was taken in 1960 at the Sand Hills Quarter Horse Show in Odessa, Tex., where Poco Pine stood grand champion stallion. Owner Paul Curtner, Jacksboro, Tex., receives the trophy from Ralph Morrison. **Photo by James Cathey**

5 POCO TIVIO

He wanted the challenge of a tough cow.

POCO BUENO had so many good sons, as well as daughters, that it's difficult to single out just a few. But without a doubt Poco Tivio was one of his very best sons. He was successful at halter and in the cutting pen, and became an outstanding sire, especially of broodmares. When Poco

Poco Tivio was a tremendous athlete and broodmare sire. This photograph was probably taken when he was about 3 years old. **Photo by James Cathey**

Tivio daughters were bred to Doc Bar, it was a magic cross—producing such horses as Doc's Oak, Doc's Remedy, Cal Bar, Boon Bar, Doc's Hotrodder, Doc's Dee Bar, and many more. Indeed, many horsemen give a lot of credit to Poco Tivio daughters for making Doc Bar so successful.

Like so many Poco Buenos, Poco Tivio was a solid bay. He was bred by E. Paul Waggoner's Three D Stock Farm in Arlington, Tex., the home of Poco Bueno. And he was foaled in 1947, out of the mare Sheilwin, who was by Pretty Boy and out of a Blackburn mare.

Foaled in 1943, Sheilwin did not attract any special attention on the Waggoner ranch until Bob Burton broke her to ride. Because she proved to be gentle and athletic, she was put into the broodmare band, where she became an outstanding producer. All of her foals were by Poco Bueno, and the first was Poco Tivio. Her second, Pretty Pokey, was foaled in 1948 and excelled in roping, reining, and working cow horse—becoming the AQHA Honor Roll Working Cow Horse in 1960.

Sheilwin's third foal was Poco Lena, one of the most outstanding mares in cutting horse history, and the dam of Doc O'Lena and Dry Doc. In 1950, Sheilwin produced Poco Champ, so named by Waggoner because he seemed so promising at birth. And he did, indeed, become an AQHA Champion, as well as a sire of AQHA Champions.

Poco Sandra was Sheilwin's 1951 foal. While this mare had limited showing in AQHA events, she had considerable success on the West Coast in open hackamore and stock horse competition. Sheilwin's

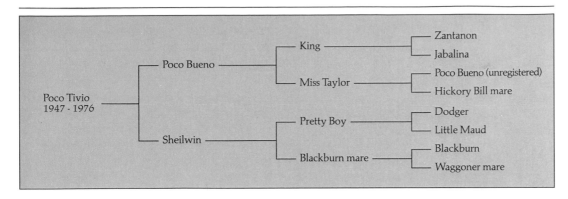

```
                                        ┌─── Zantanon
                          ┌─── King ────┤
                          │             └─── Jabalina
           ┌─ Poco Bueno ─┤
           │              │             ┌─── Poco Bueno (unregistered)
           │              └─ Miss Taylor┤
Poco Tivio │                            └─── Hickory Bill mare
1947 - 1976┤
           │                            ┌─── Dodger
           │              ┌─ Pretty Boy ┤
           │              │             └─── Little Maud
           └─── Sheilwin ─┤
                          │                  ┌─── Blackburn
                          └─ Blackburn mare ──┤
                                              └─── Waggoner mare
```

next two foals died while they were young—and she herself died at the age of 11, in 1954.

This look at Poco Tivio's siblings proves that he was no fluke; he was bred to be a great athlete and sire. He was broke on the Waggoner ranch, and started in cutting by Pine Johnson. As a 3-year-old in 1950, he was sold to Cliff Magers, an auto dealer in Fort Worth. While Magers owned the horse, Milt Bennett trained him. One year later, Don Dodge, a California trainer, bought Poco Tivio.

"Milt and I were friends," said Dodge, "and I first saw Poco Tivio through him. I bought the horse because he was good, and because there wasn't a stallion in California at that time with his breeding. That's when the Poco Bueno horses were gaining prominence.

"He was a well-mannered, extremely athletic individual," Dodge continued. "He was somewhat chunkier than today's horses, not Thoroughbred-looking, but still classy. He was easy to haul and, for me, easy to train. He was one of the best when it came to holding some of those super tough cows. As a matter of fact, he wanted the challenge of a tough cow; he never performed quite as well if the cattle were soft. He looked for a cow to make him work, but, at the same time, I never knew him to bite at a cow."

With Dodge in the saddle, Poco Tivio placed fifth in the 1951 and 1952 NCHA Top Ten. Dodge also showed the horse in reining, and Poco Tivio earned an AQHA Championship.

Dodge planned to stand Poco Tivio when he retired him from competition— and he did, for one year. "I thought I'd get

Halter and Performance Record: AQHA Champion; Halter Points, 12; Performance Points, 19; NCHA Top Ten, 1951 and '52.

Progeny Record:

AQHA Champions: 10	Performance-Point Earners: 54
Foal Crops: 25	Performance Points Earned: 1,393
Foals Registered: 308	Performance Registers of Merit: 25
Halter-Point Earners: 51	Race Starters: 0
Halter Points Earned: 463	Superior Performance Awards: 9

An early 1950s photo when Poco Tivio was named grand champion stallion at a Fort Worth-area show. He was shown by Pine Johnson.

Photo by Gressett

39

This picture was taken at Weatherford, Tex., probably around 1950, when Poco Tivio was owned by E. Paul Waggoner. The handler is Pine Johnson.

Don Dodge aboard Poco Tivio. Dodge said Poco Tivio "was one of the best when it came to holding some of those super tough cows."

rich standing him for $300," he laughed. "But one trip around was enough to put me out of the stud business. That was it." Dodge sold Poco Tivio to the renowned California horseman Charley Araujo and went back to showing—competing on Poco Lena, whom he had purchased.

Araujo stood Poco Tivio for a number of years before giving him to Floyd and Beverly Boss in 1971. Poco Tivio was then 21 years old. Floyd had shod horses for Araujo for years, and had first bred mares to Poco Tivio in 1956. Because the Bosses were sold on Poco Tivio breeding, they happily accepted when Araujo offered the old horse to them, to care for the rest of his life.

"We had a terrific veterinarian at that time," said Beverly, "and we decided to continue breeding the horse, using AI. His sperm count was extremely high, and he

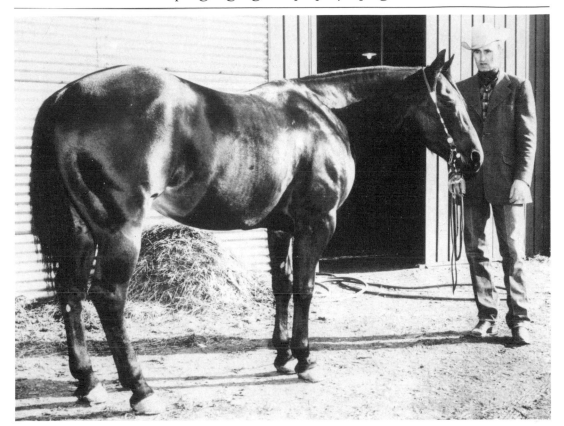

Don Dodge with Poco Tivio at Denver in 1952.

Poco Sandra, a full sister to Poco Tivio, with owner Don Dodge. This photo was taken in 1954 when Poco Sandra was named grand champion mare at the Pacific Coast Quarter Horse Association Show held at the Vessels Ranch, Los Alamitos, California.

Photo by John H. Willamson

had absolutely no trouble settling mares. We bred him until the day he died, which was in 1976. He was nearly 30 years old, and still fat and slick.

"He was really a grand horse. I was the one who cared for him, and I seldom ever needed to put a halter on him, even for clipping. I think he enjoyed all the attention." He was buried at the Boss ranch in Fresno, with a tombstone marking his grave.

"We always considered Charley a friend," Floyd pointed out. "I guess we didn't know how good a friend he was, though, until he gave us Poco Tivio. As things turned out, Charley and that horse

Monty Roberts cutting on Johnny Tivio in 1966.

Photo by Bus Jackson

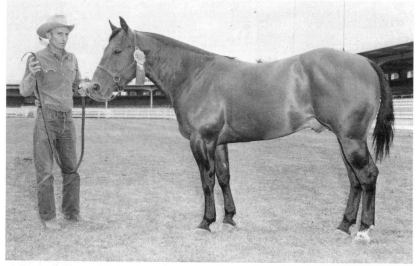

A 1953 picture of Poco Champ, a full brother to Poco Tivio, when he was named grand champion stallion at the Colorado Springs Quarter Horse show.

were two of the best friends we ever had."

As a sire, Poco Tivio proved more successful producing outstanding daughters than sons. But one of his very best offspring was Johnny Tivio, foaled in 1956,

out of the mare Chowchilla Pee Wee, and owned and shown for most of his life by Monty Roberts Jr. Roberts and his wife, Pat, own and operate a Thoroughbred farm—Flag Is Up Farms—near Solvang, California. In years past, however, Roberts was a savvy and successful competitor in West Coast horse show events.

Without being immodest, Monty said flatly that Johnny Tivio was the greatest performance horse there ever was. While some might dispute that, Johnny Tivio did, indeed, have a record that few horses have ever achieved.

For example, he was the only horse to ever win the cutting and reined cow horse in consecutive years at the famed Salinas rodeo and horse show. That was in the 1960s. One year at a Santa Barbara Quarter Horse show, also in the '60s, Monty was gunning for the all-around on Johnny. After winning the calf roping, but only placing in the reined cow horse, reining, and team roping, Monty had just the cutting left. Even if he won it, he might not have had enough points for the all-around title—so Monty entered the western riding class, even though neither

42

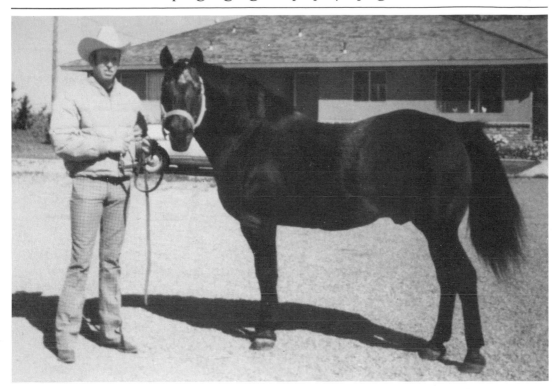

Poco Tivio at age 25, with Charlie Ward holding him.

Photo by Stephenie Ward

he nor the horse had ever ridden the pattern. Not to worry.

Monty said that immediately after marking a 74 to win the cutting, he went directly to the arena where the western riding was being held—and marked a sizzling 78, which easily won the class. Monty added, "The judge, Clyde Kennedy, said it was the most-close-to-perfect western riding run he'd ever seen." And yes, that clinched the all-around win.

Monty continued showing Johnny Tivio in western riding, competing in that event at 13 AQHA shows and winning all 13. In 1965, Johnny Tivio was the AQHA high-point stallion in western riding.

Monty also mentioned Johnny's prowess in a California all-around event called the Stallion Stakes, held in the 1960s and sponsored by Katy Peake. According to Monty, it had a sizable purse, and entries had to compete in cutting, reining, calf and team roping, reined cow horse, and pleasure. After Monty and Johnny won it 3 years in a row, Monty said the event became known as the Johnny Tivio Benefit.

Despite the success of Johnny Tivio and other sons, Poco Tivio is best remembered today through his daughters who became great producers. Take Susie's Bay, for example. Foaled in 1955, she was out of a mare named Susie L, a granddaughter of King. For years, Susie's Bay was owned by Dr. and Mrs. Stephen

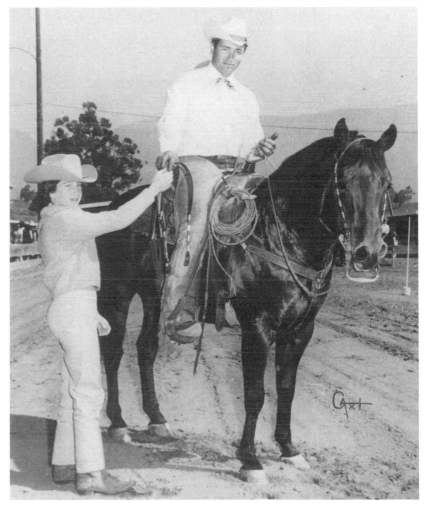

Johnny Tivio was probably Poco Tivio's best son. He's shown here with owner-rider Monty Roberts after winning the western riding class at a Santa Barbara show.

Photo by Axt

Poco Tivio cutting with Don Dodge in the saddle . . . back in the days when cutting horse riders did not hold the saddle horn.

Photo by Birdie Boyles, Courtesy of Phil Livingston

Susie's Bay, one of Poco Tivio's best-producing daughters.

Photo by Stephenie Ward

Jensen, who owned the great Doc Bar.

When bred to Doc Bar, Susie's Bay produced Doc's Marmoset, foaled in 1970, who won the NCHA Futurity and Derby, plus other major events. In 1971, she produced Doc's Solano, an outstanding performance horse and sire. In 1973, she foaled Doc's Oak, who competed and placed in both the 1976 CRCHA Snaffle Bit Futurity (for cow horses) and the NCHA Futurity. Altogether, Susie's Bay produced 12 foals by 5 stallions, who earned 1,064 AQHA points, and a huge amount of money in NCHA events.

Another great producing daughter of Poco Tivio was Teresa Tivio, foaled in 1954 out of the mare Saylor's Little Sue, by Black Hawk. When bred to Doc Bar, Teresa Tivio produced 10 foals, including Fizzabar, Nu Bar, Doc's Remedy, Boon Bar, Doc's Haida, Cal Bar, and Doc Bar Gem.

Still another terrific daughter was Jameen Tivio, foaled in 1956 out of the mare Jameen, by Jimmie Reed. Her Doc Bar foals included, among others, Doc's Hotrodder, Doc's Lynx, Doc's Tom Thumb, and Doc's Prescription.

Poco Tivio sired a total of 10 AQHA Champions, including Casey Tivio, who also earned a Superior in reining, and Old Tivio, who earned a Superior in trail horse.

With Poco Tivio's record as a sire, it's easy to see why he's still so well remembered today.

KING FRITZ

6

IT WAS 1956. Fritz and Helen Watkins of Wasco, Ore., stood looking at a 3-month-old bay colt. He was nice-looking, well-muscled, balanced, not a speck of white on him, and he had an exceptional pedigree. A double-bred King, he was sired by Power Command who was by King and out of Crickett McCue. Crickett McCue was linebred with four crosses to Jack McCue and five to Peter McCue.

The colt's dam was Poco Jane by Poco Bueno by King. Mary Jane W, Poco Jane's

"He had more athletic ability than he—or we—knew what to do with."

King Fritz as a 2-year-old, with Fritz Watkins. The bay was bred by Robert Q. Sutherland.

45

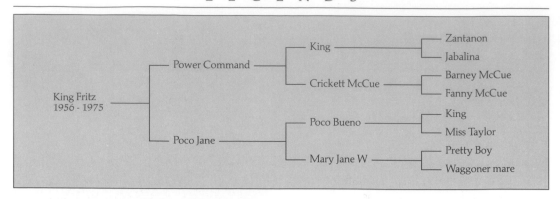

King Fritz
1956 - 1975
— Power Command
  — King
    — Zantanon
    — Jabalina
  — Crickett McCue
    — Barney McCue
    — Fanny McCue
— Poco Jane
  — Poco Bueno
    — King
    — Miss Taylor
  — Mary Jane W
    — Pretty Boy
    — Waggoner mare

Halter and Performance Record: AQHA Champion, Performance Register of Merit.

Progeny Record:

AQHA Champions: 11	Performance Points Earned: 1,786
Foal Crops: 17	Performance Registers of Merit: 51
Foals Registered: 318	Superior Halter Awards: 1
Halter-Point Earners: 35	Superior Performance Awards: 7
Halter Points Earned: 463	World Champions: 2
Performance-Point Earners: 90	

dam, was by Pretty Boy and out of a Waggoner mare.

Raymond Guthrie had purchased Poco Jane from R. Q. Sutherland of Kansas City, Missouri. At the time, Poco Jane was in foal with the bay colt. The Watkinses located him at Guthrie's place in Oregon. Mrs. Raymond Guthrie remembers Poco Jane well.

"She had that good, old foundation breeding. She was solid bay, well built, not very tall. I remember she had a big scar on her side from when she was hit by a car as a youngster."

John Ballweg, who managed R.Q. Sutherland's farm for a number of years, remembers Power Command. "Mr.

Sutherland bought him out of Texas in 1954," he recalled. "I was lucky enough to ride him to his AQHA Champion title.

"Power Command was one of those individuals who'd work as well today as he did 40 years ago. He stood 15.1, which was big in those days. He could do anything, and was about the best moving horse who ever walked. I could ride him with a full glass of water in my hand and never spill a drop. Mr. Sutherland eventually sold him back into Texas. He was only 9 when he died in 1958.

Fritz Watkins died of cancer in 1989, but Helen still has vivid recollections of the bay colt.

"My husband was raised with horses, and he grew up hearing his father tell him a good horseman could look at a 3-month-old baby and know what that same horse would look like at maturity. According to him, that 3-month-old should be a miniature version of a mature horse.

"Well, King Fritz was 3 months old when we first saw him. We bought him and two others that day for $2,000. We knew we were getting something good when we bought him, but we had no idea he'd become great. We brought him home and named him King Fritz after my husband.

"Even though it was the early 1950s, King Fritz was really a modern-type Quarter Horse. He showed a slight Thoroughbred look but, overall, he was what we always referred to as 'middle of the road.' His colts were the same way."

King Fritz had an easy disposition

and temperament. Four trainers were connected with him—Ray Junker, Buster Smith, J.L. Bartlett, and Harvey Jones. Junker was responsible for his early years.

"I got him as a 4-year-old," said Jones. "It was Buster (Smith) who broke him to ride. He'd already been shown successfully at halter, and I rode him all during his 4-year-old season.

"I can remember when we were at the Pacific International at Portland. We entered a western pleasure class and won. We thought that finished King Fritz's AQHA Championship. We left the arena thinking we were through. Well, we found out later that we still needed one-half point.

"We went through the breeding season with him and then hit the road again in May. We went to Grants Pass, Ore., and won the all-around.

"He wasn't like most stallions," Jones continued. "He never resisted anything we asked him to do, and he had more athletic ability than he—or we—knew what to do with. We showed him in cutting, working cow, reining, western pleasure. Anyone could do anything with him, and it all seemed to come easy to him.

"He was unbelievably smooth and easy to ride. He was put together just right—deep in the heart, hocks close to the ground, 1,250 pounds, a little more than 15.1. He'd still be considered modern-looking today.

"Fritz was one of those ideal horses. He did it all in the show ring and then did it all again in the breeding barn. He was a tremendous sire. His colts had his ability and disposition. They weren't extremely hot or fiery, and his daughters became great producers. I was able to show several of his offspring, and it was a real pleasure working with them."

Other trainers concur. Jack and Linda Baker of Thousand Oaks, Calif., trained the great Shirley Chex for Katherine Haley of Ventura, California. Jack, now deceased, once remarked, when talking about the King Fritzes, "They learn so quickly, they scare you."

Helen Watkins relates how the "Chex" line of horses made its debut. "Horses were a business for us. We did a lot of

King Fritz, a great sire of reining and cow horses on the West Coast.

showing and quite a bit of advertising. We wanted to come up with something that would set King Fritz's offspring, as well as our farm, apart from others.

"My husband considered using a brand that was a check mark, but then decided that wasn't too exciting. We finally decided on 'Chex.' A friend of ours once

King Fritz as a yearling.
Photo by James Cathey

Chex became a coveted name within a few short years.

told us we couldn't use it because it belonged to Ralston Purina. Well, maybe so, but they never said anything to us about it."

The Watkinses did not use the name Chex exclusively for the get of King Fritz, however. There were several stallions used in the Watkins breeding program, and their offspring also carry Chex in their names. Apparently, it was meant more as a breeding farm name than a bloodline name. But despite that, Chex has been indelibly linked with horses sired by King Fritz.

Chex became a coveted name within a few short years. Horses with that name were renowned for their abilities in the show ring, especially in reining and working cow-horse events.

In December of 1970, the Watkinses made the decision to sell King Fritz. The horse had done them a world of good, and they thought he could do the same for others.

Les Vogt, a trainer based in Clovis, Calif., and his wife, Corolynn, had watched the Chex horses win everything there was to win in the show ring. It was Shirley Chex who really got them thinking about this line of horses. When the bay mare was a 4-year-old, Ray Junker rode her at a Cow Palace horse show and won the junior reining, junior working cow horse, and junior western riding.

"He didn't just beat us a little bit," said Les, a noted reined cow-horse trainer. "He ran off with the show. The funny thing was that Ray did it all in the hackamore and he used only one hand."

Also, around that time, Bobby Ingersoll showed up with Karen Chex and Mitzi

Poco Jane, dam of King Fritz, was bred by E. Paul Waggoner. When this picture was taken, Poco Jane had won first in the 1948 mares class, but the date, location, and handler are unknown. According to one source, Poco Jane was never broke, partly because of an injury incurred as a 2-year-old, and partly because she was rather hostile to the idea.

Photo by Gressett

Power Command, sire of King Fritz, at a Dallas Quarter Horse show where he stood grand champion stallion and also won the Quarter Horse ranch riding class. The handler is John Ballweg, who now lives in Stilwell, Kansas. The date is unknown.

Photo by James Cathey

A 1958 picture of Fritz and Helen Watkins holding King Fritz (left) and Pep's Nina.

Chex. Then Katherine Haley bought Shirley Chex and put her in the hands of Jack and Linda Baker.

"Those three horses were invincible," Les said. "Wherever they were entered, you gave up thinking about winning because you couldn't. They were that strong. We'd never seen anything like it on the West Coast.

"I had never seen King Fritz, but I had a gut feeling about him and decided he was going to be great. I was 29 years old and only had $1,000 to my name, but I called up Fritz Watkins anyway and asked if the horse was for sale."

Watkins wanted $50,000 for King Fritz and another $20,000 for a band of about

10 mares that went with the stallion. So, bold as brass but poor as a church mouse, Les said he'd send $1,000 as earnest money and asked for 30 days to get the rest of the cash together.

Les owed $69,000 and didn't have a clue where to get it. But with the help and advice of a customer named Max Rouff, a good businessman who taught him financial lingo, Les talked a bank into lending him the money, using the horses as collateral.

When King Fritz arrived in California and was unloaded from the trailer, Les took one look at the much-heralded sire and said to himself, "Oh, boy, Les, what have you done?" The horse was long-haired and shaggy, and his right front foot turned out. "I never rode him but one time," Les explained. "I was afraid something would happen to him. But, he was very nice to ride, and always nice to be around."

Les soon discovered that his fears were unfounded. King Fritz stood at the White Rail Ranch in Clovis under the management of John Coffman. His stud fee was $1,000, and Les was able to pay off his bank loan in the first year. Les remembers one breeding season with over 100 mares.

"King Fritz and horses by him caught on like wildfire," he said. "They became the rage on the West Coast. If there were 10 of them in a class, they would usually take the top 10 spots. They dominated completely.

"They were so receptive to training," Les explained, "such big stoppers and great cow horses. You could make a terrible mistake in your training program with one, and the horse would forgive you and never hold it against you.

"I had my hands on a number of these horses, and when I showed, I'd win every class. I'd not only get first, I'd get first, second, and third. Being a young trainer and fairly new to the game, I wondered why the rest of the trainers could never get it together. I never realized until after King Fritz died that it was the horses. They had that much to offer a person.

"There was magic in it," Les continued. "It

A 1971 photo of Fritz Watkins (left), King Fritz, and Les Vogt when Les took delivery of the horse and gave a check to Fritz.

was so exciting to train one. You knew that every one you started was going to be great. You could visualize the great runs you were going to have on the horse and without question, you knew it would happen. And it would. They were a rare item that I've never come across since. It was a fairy tale for the 5 years I had my hands on the horse."

Then early in 1975, tragedy struck and the fairy tale turned into a nightmare.

King Fritz acted dizzy when he went to breed the first mare of the season. Local veterinarians couldn't figure out the problem, so Les had veterinarians flown in from around the nation and other countries. Money was no object for a horse who had done so much for everyone connected with him. The veterinarians diagnosed that the stallion had a damaged vertebrae near his poll, probably from an injury he had as a colt. The vertebrae developed into an extension down his spinal column, and there was no hope of repairing it. The horse had to be humanely put down at the age of 19.

"I tried to make the best of a bad situation," Les said, "but shortly after this traumatic experience, I had another one. I had 22 mares of my own in foal to King Fritz. Every mare had a claim to fame, and I thought the last foal crop should be worth a fortune. Unfortunately, that year there was a form of rhinopneumonitis going around that you couldn't vaccinate against. Twenty mares aborted."

The double blow that the death of

Early in 1975, tragedy struck and the fairy tale turned into a nightmare.

The King Fritz horses had an incredible ability to break in the loin and get in the ground. This is a 1970s photo of Les Vogt on Royal Chex, owned by Linda Keele of Santa Ynez, California. Les says that Royal Chex won every major West Coast show at least once, and adds, "He was really sensational, and was truly a favorite great horse." **Photo by Fallaw**

The King Fritz horses were tremendous cow horses and dominated the reined cow-horse events on the West Coast for years. This is Shirley Chex, ridden by Linda Baker and owned by Katherine Haley of Ventura, California. The photo was taken in 1968 at Monterey. Shirley Chex was the AHSA Champion Stock Horse 2 years in a row. **Photo by Fallaw**

King Fritz and the aborting mares dealt Les was more than he wanted to handle. On top of that, he and Corolynn divorced. They had a complete dispersal the year after King Fritz died. Strangely enough, the horses didn't bring high prices. However, in the years since, performance horse enthusiasts, especially reiners and cutters, have rediscovered the magic about King Fritz and have actively sought out King Fritz daughters to add to their breeding programs.

"The daughters are great producers," Les said, "even if they weren't top performers themselves.

"As for his sons, they didn't sire on the same level King Fritz did. Bueno Chex came the closest. He was runner-up to his dad."

According to Les, the mares he purchased from Watkins were the real key to King Fritz's success.

"Many of the mares had bloodlines that weren't well known," said Les. "Some of the best producers were by Billy Lenart, who was by Tough Company. However, Tough Company's sire was the famed Chicaro Bill and he was out of Panzarita. I did some research and found out that Billy Lenart had stood in Montana. All the people I talked to referred to horses with that breeding as ranch and rope horses. They were just big, tough horses. They weren't show horses by any means. There was another horse called Moon Hancock, also by Tough Company. He sired Moon Fin, the dam of Moon Chex. Tony Amaral had Moon Chex and I bought him for a customer. The horse was unbelievably great. So, sight unseen, I bought all the Moon Hancock mares I could find."

Ottilie and Wilma Ray, both mares by Billy Lenart, are two good examples of the magic cross with King Fritz. Ottilie produced Shirley Chex, Karen Chex, and Fritzi Chex. Wilma Ray produced Maxi Chex, Wrangler Chex, and Winema Chex—all show-ring stars.

"The broodmares I bought with these bloodlines were common-looking," Les commented. "For example, when Ottilie moved out across the pasture, her legs looked like egg beaters. She had no cadence, no coordination. None of the mares had any style to them, but they crossed exceptionally well on King Fritz.

"The ironic thing was that during the

Here are 10 outstanding horses sired by King Fritz, and equally outstanding trainer-riders. From left: Karen Chex and Lou Silva, Fritz Command Chex and Smokey Pritchett, Brassy Chex and Bobby Ingersoll, Jabalina Chex and Benny Guitron, Tangerine Chex and Duane Pettibone, Mitzi Chex and Jim Paul, Sable Command Chex and Corolynn Vogt, Astro Chex with unidentified rider, Bob Chex and Les Vogt, and Shirley Chex and Linda Baker. The picture was taken in the 1970s.

Photo by Bill McNabb, Courtesy of Les Vogt

years I had him, King Fritz was exposed to many of the greatest mares in the country, mares that were real achievers. But the King Fritz/Billy Lenart/Tough Company cross was the magic cross and it never got any better, not even when he was crossed with Doc Bar mares. There were other bloodlines that crossed well, but this was the only real strong, consistent cross."

In all, King Fritz sired 11 AQHA Champions, 3 Superior western pleasure horses, 3 Superior reiners, 1 Superior in cutting, 1 Superior in halter, and 51 show ROMs.

It should be noted, however, that many of King Fritz's sons and daughters were shown on the West Coast in open stock horse and reined cow horse competition. Although they dominated this competition, especially in the 1970s, they received no AQHA recognition or points. If they had, King Fritz would have a far more impressive AQHA record as a sire.

7

THREE BARS (TB)

VEGAS
GREAT GREAT
GRANDFATHER

3 SOCKS
GREAT GREAT GREAT
GRANDFATHER

Three Bars has had the greatest impact on the Quarter Horse breed of any horse in history.

3 SOCKS
GREAT GREAT
GRANDFATHER

WITHOUT A shadow of a doubt, Three Bars has had the greatest impact on the Quarter Horse breed of any horse in history. Some might dispute this statement, but not very many. Just take a look at Three Bars' record as a sire. Whereas most great stallions dominate just one phase of the industry, Three Bars forever left his mark in racing, halter, cutting, and other arena performance events.

In racing, just a very few of his superstar offspring included Goldseeker Bars, Mr. Bar None, Rocket Bar, Three Chicks, The Ole Man, Pokey Bar, Josie's Bar, Mr Bruce, Sugar Bars, Kid Meyers, St. Bar, Lightning Bar, Barred, Bob's Folly, Galobar, Breeze Bar, and Little Lena's Bar. Altogether,

Three Bars sired 317 foals who earned their ROM in racing, and 38 who earned a Superior in racing. When his daughter Lena's Bar (TB) was bred to Jet Deck, the resulting foal was the phenomenal Easy Jet.

In halter, will there ever be another sire to equal the record of Impressive? Impressive was by Lucky Bar (TB), by Three Bars, and out of a Three Bars granddaughter. But before Impressive came along, there was Steel Bars, who sired many fine halter horses, including Aledo Bar, the 1959 AQHA high-point halter stallion.

In cutting, Doc Bar revolutionized the industry. Doc Bar was a grandson of Three Bars, and his record as a sire of cutters may also never be equaled.

Sid Vail with Three Bars, circa 1961.

Photo by Orren Mixer

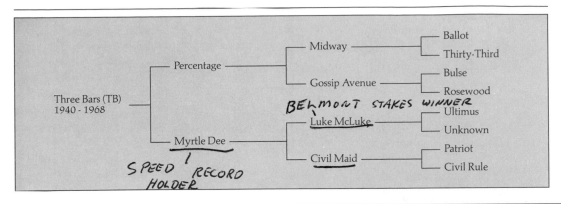

Three Bars (TB)
1940 - 1968

Percentage
- Midway
  - Ballot
  - Thirty-Third
- Gossip Avenue
  - Bulse
  - Rosewood

Myrtle Dee
- Luke McLuke *[BELMONT STAKES WINNER]*
  - Ultimus
  - Unknown
- Civil Maid
  - Patriot
  - Civil Rule

SPEED RECORD HOLDER

In reining, roping, and other arena events, a host of Three Bars get and grandget excelled as sires and producers. Sugar Bars, for example, sired 30 AQHA Champions, back in the days when that was a coveted title. Another son, Parr Three, earned a Superior at halter—and then sired the great Zan Parr Bar.

Reams of copy could be devoted to the achievements of this sire's descendants, but let's take a look at Three Bars himself.

Foaled in 1940, he was by Percentage, who was a stakes winner. Percentage's dam, Gossip Avenue, produced eight foals, with seven of them being winners on the track. Gossip Avenue's sire, Bulse, made a name for himself as an outstanding sprinter. Gossip Avenue's dam, Rosewood, produced seven winners, including two stakes winners.

The dam of Three Bars was Myrtle Dee, a speedburner who once set a record for 5½ furlongs at an Ohio track. She came by her speed honestly as her sire, Luke McLuke, won the Belmont Stakes in 1914, and her dam, Civil Maid, was a granddaughter of Ben Brush, who won the Kentucky Derby in 1896.

When Myrtle Dee was 16 and in foal to Percentage, she was purchased at a sale, as part of a package of several mares, by three men: Jack Goode, Ned Brent, and Bill Talbot. She was turned out on Brent's farm in Kentucky's Bourbon County, and foaled Three Bars on April 8, 1940.

Because the chestnut colt was such a good-looking fellow and was bred to run, the owners thought they had hit the jackpot. So they named him Three Bars, after the three bars in slot machines.

When the colt was 2, it looked as if the men had, indeed, hit the jackpot. Three

Bars could break from the gate and cover 440 yards like a speeding bullet. But then, trouble. In 1968, *Horseman* magazine published an article which included the following comments from Goode.

"In the spring of his 2-year-old year, I was bringing him off the track one morning when his hind leg turned ice cold, just like you had suddenly turned off the blood. He never got over it while we owned him. Until that happened, he was the fastest thing I had put a bridle on. He was too rapid. You had to ease him off slow or he'd get out of hand and you couldn't handle him well. I took him to Keeneland and to Detroit, but never raced him because that leg would get cold when he exerted himself. We had some of the best vets in Kentucky work with Three

"He was the fastest thing I had put a bridle on."

— VEGAS!!

According to Walter Merrick, Three Bars stood about 15.3 hands.

Photo by Orren Mixer

Another photograph of Sid Vail with Three Bars.   **Photo by Orren Mixer**

Bars, but they couldn't help that leg.

"Later on, they found that condition happened to horses when bloodworms clogged an artery and cut off circulation. After a while the leg would be okay. Maybe the next day it would be fine . . . then Three Bars could run."

Goode, Brent, and Talbot decided, however, to sell the horse—and they sold him to Beckham Stivers for $300. But it was stipulated that Stivers didn't have to pay unless Three Bars won a race; then the $300 would be taken out of the purse. Goode, Brent, and Talbot never got their $300, and Three Bars was eventually sold again.

After a couple of more owners, and after winning a couple of races, Three Bars was entered in a $2,000 claiming race in Detroit. And he was claimed. Some reports say he was claimed by trainer Cal Kennedy for Stan Snedigar; other reports say that Kennedy, Snedigar, and Toad Haggard claimed him as a partnership. Whichever, the horse was shipped to the Phoenix area, with the intention of breeding him to Quarter racing mares. At that time, southern Arizona was a hotbed of short-horse racing.

Three Bars had not been in Arizona very long, however, before a cowboy named Sid Vail heard about him. Sid and his wife, Mayola, had a small cow ranch out of Douglas, Ariz., and whenever they got a few dollars saved, Sid looked for a fast horse or two, according to an article in *Western Horseman*, December 1963, by Ed Ellinger. Because Vail had a couple of

Although Three Bars was probably never a saddle horse per se, evidently Vail would occasionally saddle him up for a ride on the ranch.

Photos by Orren Mixer

mares he wanted to breed, he went up to Phoenix to take a look at Three Bars.

Ellinger wrote: "Three Bars was in his stall when Sid first set eyes on him. His reaction was immediate, and he recalls it with great clarity. 'I never pictured a horse that could look that good. If there was ever a perfect horse, he was it. I couldn't fault him anywhere.'"

Vail immediately offered the owner(s) $5,000 for the horse, but it was turned down. Vail returned to his ranch, but could think of nothing but Three Bars. He was determined to own him. He finally returned to Phoenix with an offer of $10,000, and this time was successful in buying the horse.

According to Ellinger, Vail decided to let Melville Haskell stand Three Bars at his ranch close to Tucson. Sid agreed to pay Haskell $30 a month to care for the horse; Haskell would get the board payments on mares brought to the ranch to be bred to Three Bars; and Vail would get the $100 stud fee. That was in 1945.

By early 1946, the horse had completely recovered from his leg problems, and Vail wanted to race the horse to build his reputation. He leased him to Kennedy, Haggard, and Snedigar, who agreed to run the horse.

Ellinger wrote: "Three Bars really burned up the tracks. He doubtless was the fastest horse in the United States for 5 furlongs. He broke the track record at Phoenix, for that distance, in 57.3. Then at Agua Caliente was clocked at a blistering 56.4 for

Mr. Bar None, out of Murl L. by Moco Burnett, was another popular and successful son of Three Bars. Foaled in 1955 and bred, owned, and trained by Oscar Jeffers Jr., he was Champion Quarter Running 2-Year-Old in 1957 and World Champion Quarter Running Horse in 1958.

Photo by Jack Stribling

the first 5 furlongs in a 6-furlong race."

Because of Three Bars' sizzling early speed, he was tiring before reaching the more typical Thoroughbred distances. (One furlong is ⅛ of a mile.) According to several stories, Three Bars' trainer tried to rate him back a little by putting a bicycle

Gay Widow, by King P-234 and out of Happy Gal, produced Gay Bar King, by Three Bars. This picture was taken at the 1953 Jacksboro, Tex., Quarter Horse show where Gay Widow was grand champion mare and first in junior reining. She was owned by Julia Reed, Meridian, Texas.

Photo by James Cathey

Gay Bar King, by Three Bars and out of Gay Widow, was foaled in 1958, and became a successful sire of performance horses.

chain across his nose, but the effort backfired because thereafter the horse absolutely refused to be rated.

When Three Bars was retired again, few Quarter mares were brought to his court when he stood at Vail's ranch near Douglas from 1947 to 1951. Then in 1952, Vail leased the horse to Walter Merrick, Sayre, Okla., for 2 years.

Merrick, of course, has been one of the greatest breeders of Quarter running horses in history. He has also been one of the industry's greatest visionaries. Back in the 1940s, he had accumulated a number of good mares, and was looking for a Thoroughbred stallion to cross on them.

In 1949, Merrick was in southern Arizona at the Rillito racetrack. One day in the track kitchen, he was visiting with a border patrolman, R.G. "Mitch" Mitchelena, who was a frequent visitor to the kitchen. Merrick no sooner mentioned to Mitch that he was looking for a good Thoroughbred stallion when Mitch said, "Come with me." Mitch drove Merrick to Vail's ranch, and as soon as Merrick saw

Lightning Bar, a 1951 son of Three Bars and Della P, earned a AAA rating on the track and an AQHA Championship. He went on to become a very successful sire. He's shown here with owner Art Pollard at the 1955 Sonoita, Ariz., Quarter Horse show where he was grand champion stallion.

**Photo by
Richard Schaus**

Three Bars, he knew he had found the right horse.

In Lyn Jank's book, *The Quarter Horse, That Special Breed*, Merrick is quoted:

"The first time I looked at Three Bars, I knew he was the one I wanted. He wasn't a big horse. He had the right bone structure, and the conformation that could give a Quarter Horse a little more reach, a little more refinement. You could look in his eyes and know his disposition, and know he wasn't a horse that was going to cause any problems."

Merrick wanted to buy the horse immediately, especially when he learned of his blazing early speed.

But, Vail did not want to sell the horse, and it took Merrick several years just to get him leased. Vail finally agreed to lease him for 2 years when he admitted that Three Bars had not been getting too many mares, possibly because of the ranch's remote location, and Merrick said he thought he could fill the horse's book in Oklahoma.

So Three Bars was taken to Oklahoma—amidst a storm of controversy. At that time, the AQHA was under siege from breeders who wanted to keep Thoroughbred blood out, and from breeders like Merrick who thought

Sugar Bars, one of Three Bars' very best sons, was out of Frontera Sugar. He was AAA on the track, and became a leading sire of race colts and AQHA Champions. This picture was taken in 1956 at Enid, Okla., where he was reserve champion stallion. The handler is Bud Warren.

Joan, one of Walter Merrick's broodmares, was by Joe Hancock. When she was bred to Midnight Jr., she produced Hot Heels, and when bred to Three Bars, produced Steel Bars.

Photo Courtesy of Walter Merrick

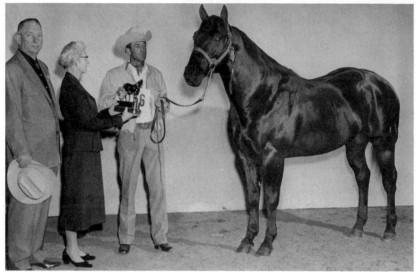

Steel Bars, by Three Bars and out of Joan, earned more fame in the show ring and as a leading sire of AQHA Champions than he did on the track. This picture was taken at the 1957 Houston Livestock Show where he was grand champion stallion. Left to right are Lester Goodson, Mrs. Gus Scroggins, and Matlock Rose. **Photo by James Cathey**

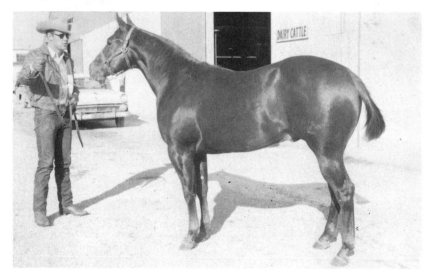

One of Steel Bars' best sons was Aledo Bar, foaled in 1957 and out of Willful Miss, by King P-234. He was an AQHA Champion and a leading sire of AQHA Champions. This 1959 photo shows John Payne at the halter.

infusions of Thoroughbred blood would be good for Quarter Horses.

"That was kind of a tough time with the association," remembered Merrick. "There had been a split in AQHA, and some of us went into the National Quarter Horse Breeders Association. In 1952, the majority of AQHA members were saying no to Thoroughbreds.

"I didn't care. I believed in Three Bars from the first time I saw him. I knew he'd work on my Joe Hancock and Midnight Jr. mares. Those first foals went to the track in '55, and one of them was Bob's Folly, who became a AAAT stakes winner. He was out of Hot Heels, a Midnight Jr. mare."

Before Merrick leased Three Bars, the horse had already sired Bardella, who was foaled in 1950, out of the mare Della P, by Doc Horn (TB). Bardella, rated AAAT, became Champion Quarter Running 2-Year-Old and 3-Year-Old Filly. Della P was bred right back to Three Bars and the result was Lightning Bar, foaled in 1951. Rated AAA on the track, he became an AQHA Champion and a leading sire, and leading maternal grandsire, of ROM race horses. His most famous son, however, was Doc Bar, who couldn't outrun a fat porcupine, but who still went on to fame and fortune.

Even though Three Bars was relatively unknown in Oklahoma and Texas, Merrick had no trouble filling his book with 70 mares at a $300 stud fee. Evidently many breeders figured that if Merrick liked the horse, that was good enough for them.

Although Vail had agreed to lease Three Bars to Merrick for 2 years, he changed his mind after that first year and wanted the horse back. Merrick explained that in

St. Bar, a 1963 son of Three Bars out of Bella St. Mary, by Spotted Bull (TB). He was AAAT and an AQHA Champion. He was shown by George Tyler to the grand champion stallion title at Houston in 1968. Others shown, from left: L.M. Pearce Jr., president of the Houston Livestock Show & Rodeo; Don Jones, AQHA executive secretary; and Mr. and Mrs. L.M. French Jr. of Odessa, Tex., owners of the stallion.

Photo by Keeland

those days, he did business on a hand-shake, so he had nothing in writing verifying his 2-year-lease agreement with Vail. When Merrick offered to buy the horse, Vail priced him at $50,000, well beyond what Merrick could afford.

By this time, the Vails had moved to a place near Tucson, and Sid wanted the horse back to breed to his own mares. So that's where Three Bars stood in 1953, 1954, and 1955, and that's where Merrick hauled his mares.

According to Ellinger's article in *Western Horseman*, later in the 1950s, Vail moved to California where Quarter Horse racing was growing at a more rapid rate than in Arizona. And more and more breeders were taking their mares to Three Bars, whose stud fee eventually reached $10,000. If you wanted a race horse in those days, you bred to Three Bars or one of his good sons. Even though Three Bars' stud fee was expensive, the resulting foals were selling for two, three, four, and five times the fee.

From their first California location in Apple Valley, the Vails moved to a 900-acre ranch in the central part of the state, near Oakdale. They named the ranch— what else?—the Three Bars Ranch.

As the years passed, Merrick continually hauled his mares out to California, to be bred. But in 1967, when Three Bars was 27 years old, Vail agreed to let Merrick

Another outstanding Three Bars grandson was Tonto Bars Hank, by Tonto Bars Gill. Foaled in 1958, Tonto Bars Hank won the All-American Futurity in 1960, was the champion Quarter running stallion as both a 2-year-old and 3-year-old, and became a leading sire of ROM race colts. He was owned by C.G. Whitcomb of Sterling, Colo., and his rider here is Celie Whitcomb at age 11.   **Photo by Jack Stribling**

If you wanted a race horse in those days, you bred to Three Bars or one of his good sons.

Rapid Bar, a 1958 son of Three Bars and out of Miss Chicaro, by Chicaro Bill. He was AAAT and an AQHA Champion, and sired a number of ROM race colts. Shown (left to right) are Joe Hutchinson, Colorado Springs; Reed Hill of Canadian, Tex.; and Doc Hutchinson of Colorado Springs.

Photo by Darol Dickinson

Lightning Rey, by Lightning Bar and out of Reina Rey by Rey, was typical of many of Three Bars' outstanding grandsons. Foaled in 1958, he was AAA, a Supreme Champion, and an AQHA Champion. This photo was taken at Prescott, and the rider is Dwight Stewart.

Photo by Johnny Johnston

take the horse back to Oklahoma, and keep him for the rest of his life.

Merrick said he was in California at a horse sale, where Sid and Mayola also happened to be. After they exchanged howdies, Merrick said he noticed Sid and Mayola spent a lot of time with their heads together, in a serious discussion. Finally Sid walked up to Merrick and asked if they could meet with him . . . and that's when Sid offered Three Bars to him. Vail assured Merrick that despite Three Bars' age, he was still breeding and settling mares, and Vail's veterinarian later confirmed this.

Merrick, of course, was thrilled to get Three Bars back. As to why Vail agreed to let the horse go, Merrick believes it was because he loved the old horse so much, he couldn't bear the thought of being with him when he finally passed on. That, coupled with the fact he knew Merrick would give the horse excellent care, apparently led to his decision.

But, there was one stipulation to the deal. Merrick also had to take Three Bars' inseparable companion, a blind mare named Fairy Adams. Three Bars, always a gentle horse, had struck up a friendship with the mare several years prior to 1967. At first, it was an over-the-fence friendship, but as it grew, Vail finally had to let the pair stay together because Three Bars was prone to tantrums when the mare was out of his sight.

Merrick agreed to take Fairy Adams, and kept them in adjoining stalls, with

The great Rocket Bar, a Thoroughbred son of Three Bars out of Golden Rocket, was a leading sire of ROM race colts.

Photo by Darol Dickinson

a large opening cut into the partition between them.

It was the end of March 1968 when Three Bars died. He had a number of mares settled and in foal when he suffered a heart attack.

By that time, Vail had moved to a ranch at Nocona, Texas. When Merrick called to tell him that the horse had died, Vail asked if Merrick could bring the horse down to Nocona for burial, which he did. But shortly after that, Vail pulled up stakes and moved back to California. Merrick wishes that he had been able to bury Three Bars on his 14 Ranch at Sayre, but he deferred to Vail's request to bury the horse in Nocona.

Some may question if animals can grieve, but there was no question that Fairy Adams was desolate after Three Bars died. She was unusually quiet, and refused to leave her stall unless someone took her for a walk. She produced her last foal by Three Bars in 1969, a colt Merrick named The Last Son. Fairy Adams died in 1971. When she did, Merrick's wife, Tina, was relieved because, as she said, "The guardian angel of horses was knocking a hole between two stalls so Fairy Adams and Three Bars could be together again."

Bar Money, by Three Bars and out of Miss Ruby, by Los Molinos (TB), being shown in western pleasure by Tommy Manion at Denver in 1967. Foaled in 1960, Bar Money was AAA, an AQHA Champion and Supreme Champion, and a leading sire of ROM race and arena colts.

8

DOC BAR

He was a good halter horse and an extraordinary sire whose get totally transformed the sport of cutting.

DOC BAR will forever be remembered as the horse who revolutionized the cutting horse industry. But, he was not bred to be a cow horse. A look at his pedigree shows speed, and that's what Tom and Jack Finley of Gilbert, Ariz., wanted when they bred Dandy Doll to Lightning Bar, a AAA AQHA Champion son of Three Bars (TB).

Dandy Doll was a AA mare by Texas Dandy, an athletic horse who sired 14 AAA runners and 3 AQHA Champions. Tom Finley says, "Dandy Doll won races from 220 yards up to 440 yards. She was a small mare with a lot of guts."

By crossing two running bloodlines, the Finleys had high hopes for a speedster.

"We wanted a race horse from that breeding," said Tom Finley (a past president of the AQHA), "but we didn't get a race horse. What we got was a good-looking horse who did well at halter."

At 14.3 and 1,000 pounds, Doc Bar didn't look the part of a stretchy, streamlined race horse. He was a washout on the racetrack, earning only $95 in four starts.

Art Pollard, who owned Lightning Bar,

Doc Bar as a 3-year-old in 1959.

Photo by Western Livestock Journal

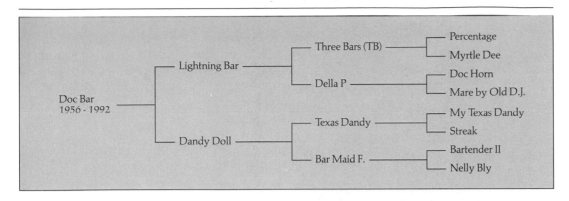

remembers Doc Bar's racing debut as a 2-year-old at Rillito Park in Tucson. In an article about Doc Bar in *Cutting Horse* (February 1992), author Sally Harrison quoted Pollard as follows:

"The gate opened and he broke and ran about 50 yards and came in last by about 10 lengths. After the race, Tom and Jack asked me if I would give $1,000 for him, which was about what they had in him with the stud fee, raising him, and this race. They didn't know what to do with him. I said I wouldn't give my pocket-knife. He wasn't my type. So two fools met—they were fool enough to offer him and I was fool enough to refuse."

Doc Bar was not a race horse. He wasn't even a performance horse. But he turned out to be a good halter horse and an extraordinary sire whose get totally transformed the sport of cutting. And although he was never ridden in competition, his sons and daughters forever changed the cutting horse industry with their ability and style. They've not only found their way into the cutting arena, but other performance events as well—such as working cow horse, reining, and western pleasure.

Charley Araujo, from Coalinga, Calif., was a good friend of the Finleys. He had seen Doc Bar when the stocking-legged colt was still nursing his mother, and remarked to the Finleys that he'd like to show the horse at halter if he didn't make a runner. Araujo got his wish, and also convinced the Finleys to let him stand Doc Bar in California. He showed the horse at halter 13 times, earning 36 points, with 12 wins and 1 second. Doc Bar also stood grand champion 10 times and reserve champion once.

Doc Bar culminated his halter career in 1962 at the Cow Palace in San Francisco, where he was named grand champion

Halter and Performance Record: Halter Points, 36; Race Winnings, $95.

Progeny Record:

AQHA Champions: 27	Race Starters: 7
Foal Crops: 19	Performance-Point Earners: 207
Foals Registered: 485	Performance Points Earned: 4,569.5
Halter-Point Earners: 101	Performance Registers of Merit: 118
Halter Points Earned: 2,492	Superior Halter Awards: 9
Race Money Earned: $1,098	Superior Performance Awards: 20
Race Registers of Merit: 1	World Champions: 2
Leading Race Money Earner: Tripolay Bar ($495)	

stallion; his son, Barlet, was reserve champion; and his daughter, Janie Bar, was reserve champion mare.

This caught the attention of a dentist and his wife who lived near the San Francisco Bay area. Dr. and Mrs. Stephen Jensen of Orinda bought the 6-year-old stallion from the Finleys for $30,000 in 1962. In those days, that was an impressive price.

"Charley Araujo thought of him as nothing more than a pretty halter horse," says Stephenie Jensen Ward, the Jensens' daughter. "He rode him once or twice, and swore the horse couldn't even change leads and wasn't at all athletic.

"He'd already sired some top halter horses by the time my parents bought him," Stephenie continued, "so he was too valuable as a sire to take out and train."

The Jensens had purchased a 680-acre ranch in Paicines, Calif., in 1958, and they called the ranch the Double J.

"They didn't know a thing about raising horses when they bought the ranch," Stephenie smiled. "They talked about

Charley Araujo thought of him as nothing more than a pretty halter horse.

Charlie and Stephenie Ward with Doc Bar in a 1977 photo.

Photo by Pat Close

Doc Bar had a classy head.

whether they wanted to buy cattle or horses, and decided foals would look prettier than calves in the pastures. They started talking to people in the horse business, and did some reading. They listened and learned before they began buying.

"None of us had any idea what was going to happen when Doc Bar became a part of our family. We thought he was an outstanding individual, but we certainly never dreamed of how things would turn out.

"His success as a halter sire was immediate. Then, after a few years, halter horse conformation started getting more Thoroughbred-looking. That wasn't Doc, and during that period he didn't breed a lot of mares."

So, here was a race-bred horse who couldn't run. He supposedly wasn't athletic and couldn't change leads. Now his conformation was starting to fall out of favor in the halter world. What was left for him?

"Mom and Dad had bought some Poco Tivio mares," Stephenie continued. "They preferred the working-type Poco Tivios, and had about three from Charley, who also stood Poco Tivio at that time. Then, they decided to cross those mares on Doc. They were short, fat, brown things, and people wondered why they were crossing

Lightning Bar, the sire of Doc Bar, in a photo taken at the 1954 Tucson Quarter Horse show, where he was the reserve champion stallion. Owner Art Pollard showed him.

Photo by Matt Culley

them on a classy halter horse."

However, the Doc Bar-Poco Tivio cross became one of the greatest nicks in Quarter Horse history. An example of the magic cross was Fizzabar, a 1961 mare by Doc Bar and out of Teresa Tivio. "Fizzabar made a name for herself as a California reined cow horse when Harry Rose was riding her," said Stephenie. "Then Don Dodge took her and made her into a spectacular cutting horse. She wound up in the NCHA Hall of Fame." And in 1968, with Dodge in the saddle, Fizzabar became the National Cutting Horse Association World Champion Mare. Other good horses Teresa Tivio produced by Doc Bar are Cal Bar, Nu Bar, Doc's Remedy, Doc's Haida, Boon Bar, and Doc Bar Gem.

Another Poco Tivio daughter was Susie's Bay, described by Stephenie as "a great big old tank of a mare." When bred to Doc Bar, she produced Doc's Marmoset, winner of the '73 NCHA Futurity; Doc's Solano, youngest horse to ever win

Doc Bar as a 6-year-old when the Jensens bought him in 1962.

The Doc Bar dynasty in the cutting world began in 1969.

an AQHA Championship; Doc's Bar Bender, a great calf roping horse; and Doc's Oak, a finalist in both the 1976 NCHA Futurity and the CRCHA Snaffle Bit Futurity (for reined cow horses).

Besides Poco Tivio daughters, the Jensens also had daughters of other foundation-bred Quarter Horses, such as King P-234, Leo, and Hollywood Gold.

The Doc Bar dynasty in the cutting world began in 1969, with four offspring entered in the NCHA Futurity. Three placed second through fourth: Doc's Kitty, ridden by Shorty Freeman; Doc Luck Bar, ridden by Buster Welch; and Doc's Leo Lad, ridden by Carol Rose.

A unprecedented string of NCHA Futurity wins continued almost unbroken for 2 decades, in which Doc Bar's get and

grandget dominated cutting's most prestigious event.

In 1970, Doc O'Lena, ridden by Freeman, won all four go-rounds of the NCHA Futurity, a record that still stands as this is written. In 1971, Dry Doc, ridden by Welch, claimed the crown. Both stallions were out of Poco Lena, a famous cutting mare sired by Poco Bueno.

In 1973, Doc's Marmoset, ridden by Tom Lyons, won, followed by Doc's Yuba Lea, ridden by Leon Harrel, in 1974.

In 1975, Lenaette, a daughter of Doc O'Lena, won, making her a Doc Bar second-generation NCHA Futurity winner. She was ridden by Shorty Freeman.

The wins picked up again in 1978 with Lynx Melody, ridden by Larry Reeder; in 1979 with Docs Diablo, ridden by Bill Freeman (Shorty's son); and in 1980 Mis Royal Mahogany, ridden by Lindy Burch. All three were Doc Bar grandget.

Then, in 1982, another Doc O'Lena won the NCHA Futurity. Smart Little

Lena, ridden by Bill Freeman, went on to win the NCHA triple crown: NCHA Futurity, NCHA Derby, and NCHA Super Stakes. In 1987 and 1988, two of Smart Little Lena's get earned victories in the NCHA Futurity, making them the only futurity winners whose sire and grandsire were both futurity winners. In 1987, it was Smart Date, with Leon Harrel in the saddle, and in 1988, it was Smart Little Senor, with Bill Freeman riding.

The ability of Doc Bar and his sons and daughters to pass on their talents was never more evident than in the 1983 NCHA Futurity, when 21 of the 23 finalists had Doc Bar somewhere in their bloodlines, either on the paternal or maternal side.

All this time, Doc Bar never left the Double J, whose name was changed to the Doc Bar Ranch in the 1970s. His sons, daughters, and grandget made his name for him, and it was only fitting to name the ranch after him. The ranch, about 45 minutes south of Hollister, Calif., is managed by Stephenie and her husband, Charlie Ward. Charlie took over management of Doc Bar in 1963.

According to AQHA records, Doc Bar sired 485 foals who earned 2,492 halter points and 4,569.5 performance points. Twenty-seven became AQHA Champions. While that's an impressive record, it does not truly reflect his greatness as a sire because many of his sons and daughters competed only in NCHA cuttings, not AQHA events.

Nor is there an accurate count of the hundreds of thousands of dollars his offspring won, or of the dozens of breeders and trainers who became successful in the horse business by owning, training, or showing Doc Bar offspring.

At the age of 21, the grand old horse sired his last foal, aptly named Doc's Last Chance, who was born in 1978. Sterile by that time, Doc Bar spent the remainder of his years in pasture with a favorite old mare.

Doc Bar was 36 years old when he was humanely put down on July 20, 1992. Charlie and Stephenie made the painful decision after it was obvious the old horse

One of the most frequently used photographs of Doc Bar.

was no longer able to digest his food properly. He couldn't maintain his weight and was having trouble getting up. His grave is under a black walnut tree in a pasture. But while his death marked the end of the grand stallion's life, his legend and his gift to the cutting world lives on.

"Doc really revolutionized the cutting world in terms of looks and action," says

Malcolm Chartier cutting on Dry Doc, full brother to Doc O'Lena. Chartier, who lives in Fair Haven, Mich., bought Dry Doc as a 2-year-old from the Jensens, right after Doc O'Lena won the 1970 NCHA Futurity. He put Dry Doc in training with Buster Welch, who won the '71 Futurity with the horse. Dry Doc has changed owners several times since, and is currently owned by the Hanley Ranch in Lincoln, California.

Photo by Dalco

A 1977 photo of Dry Doc when Chartier still owned him.

Photo by Anna Foote

Stephenie. "His colts were prettier with keener heads and better necks than the more old-style types who preceded him."

Doc Bar stood 14.3 and weighed about 1,000 pounds, and many of his offspring were of a similar size, or even smaller. But a horse doesn't need size for quickness or athletic ability, and the Doc Bars were loaded with swiftness, agility, and style, plus class, cowiness, and charisma.

However, they were not all the same. Charlie Ward put it this way: "Some had more ability than others, and some were a little more high-strung than others. I had the most success with ones that were just a little bit hot. But being hot didn't mean they were crazy; there is a difference.

"With some, you found out right away they had the ability and the *cow* that it takes, and sometimes they were liable to overreact at first. I still remember the first few times I took Doc's Starlight into the arena with cattle. She didn't know what I

The great cutting mare Poco Lena, with Don Dodge. Poco Lena produced just two foals, Doc O'Lena and Dry Doc, both by Doc Bar. In her lifetime, Poco Lena had several owners, including Dodge.

wanted because she had no experience, and she was a little wild at first. It took awhile, but I finally got her calmed down so she would make just one move instead of five. When she got the idea, it was set in her mind. Then she was sure one of those horses that, when you were in tough competition and the cattle got bad, and you knew the only way you could win was to really ask her . . . she always had that extra and would come through for you."

Doc Bar is credited with bringing a totally different look to cutting horses, and for putting the sweeping motion into the cutting horses of today. And his get loved to cut . . . to toy with a cow just the way a cat will toy with a mouse. They enjoyed the challenge of going head-to-head with a wily ol' cow.

Doc Bar's get and grandget have all proven that they can pass on the greatness of "the old man." Consequently, there will always be a demand for horses of Doc Bar breeding—not just by cutting horse riders, but anyone who wants a classy, intelligent, and talented athlete.

Doc's Lynx, another outstanding son of Doc Bar, out of Jameen Tivio, by Poco Tivio. He was foaled in 1969.

Photo by Don Trout

9

BARBRA B

**Her match
race against a
Thoroughbred
stallion gained
nationwide
attention.**

THIS BAY mare gained fame as one of
the greatest Quarter running mares in the
1940s. And she carved herself a permanent niche in history when she was
matched against a Thoroughbred stallion
at Hollywood Park in 1947. But more

about that later.

Foaled in 1943, Barbra B was bred by
Roy Snow of Okmulgee, Oklahoma. She
was a pretty mare whose conformation
reflected the running blood in her background, and not the bulldog type so typi-

*Barbra B, as pictured
in the 1947 yearbook
of the AQRA.*

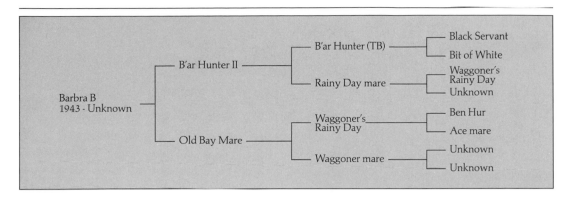

Barbra B 1943 - Unknown	B'ar Hunter II	B'ar Hunter (TB)	Black Servant
			Bit of White
		Rainy Day mare	Waggoner's Rainy Day
			Unknown
	Old Bay Mare	Waggoner's Rainy Day	Ben Hur
			Ace mare
		Waggoner mare	Unknown
			Unknown

cal of many Quarter Horses in those days. Her sire was B'ar Hunter II, who was by B'ar Hunter (TB) and out of a Quarter mare by Waggoner's Rainy Day.

As her pedigree shows, Barbra B was linebred to Waggoner's Rainy Day. This horse was used for years at the Waggoner Ranch in Electra, Texas. When he was 19, he was purchased by Art Beall of Bartlesville, Oklahoma. Beall is quoted in Nelson C. Nye's *Outstanding Modern Quarter Horse Sires* as saying, "I rate Rainy Day high as a sire because of the kind of colts he gets. They are not extreme bulldogs, nor are they of Thoroughbred appearance. They are just good-withered, well-muscled, good-headed, clean-boned colts with good feet and plenty of action. They have style and quality, as well as intelligence and toughness.

"George Humphreys, foreman of the Four Sixes, told me the Waggoners used Rainy Day horses to make the long rides and for riding the rough country at roundups. Every cowboy's string had one or two Rainy Day horses, and they were always given the rough work."

It is believed that Waggoner's Rainy Day was raced as a 2-year-old, but there is no record. However, his sire, Ben Hur, was one of the better race horses of his day, as well as a good sire.

Nye summed up his comments about Waggoner's Rainy Day by stating: "His get are most widely known for their durability and intelligence as ranch horses and for their speed on the track and elsewhere. They may not run a hole in the wind, but they'll take a man there and bring him back."

Not much is known about Barbra B's sire, B'ar Hunter II, other than the fact he

Halter and Performance Record: Racing Register of Merit; Earnings, $3,050.

Produce of Dam Record:

Barbara Tex	1952 mare by My Texas Dandy Jr. Racing Register of Merit
Pelican Gill	1954 stallion by Pelican
Barbara Grace	1957 mare by Glass Truckle (TB)
Captain Crusade	1958 stallion by Glass Truckle (TB)
Adrienne	1959 mare by Bar Tonto
Richie	1961 stallion by Glass Truckle (TB) Racing Register of Merit
Joe B Less	1965 stallion by Joe Less Racing Register of Merit

was a half-Thoroughbred. Obviously, however, he sired at least one horse that had speed to burn.

Barbra B's dam was an unbroke daughter of Waggoner's Rainy Day, who was referred to as the Old Bay Mare.

No one seems to know for sure if Barbra B was foaled in Oklahoma and taken to Gilbert, Ariz., along with her dam, as a suckling; or if she was actually foaled in Gilbert. It is a fact, however, that she was in Gilbert when she was just a few months old.

Buck Nichols, who lives in Gilbert, says: "Snow, her breeder, was a barber from Oklahoma. He moved to Arizona because he thought he had tuberculosis, and set up a barbershop. He was friends with my dad, Ab Nichols, and lived with my folks. Barbra B was about as nice a mare as I've

*This Gill Cattle Company ad in the 1947 AQRA yearbook featured their talented race mare. The photos were taken at Holly-wood Park when Barbra B won her match race with *Fair Truckle.*

BARBRA B

Bay Mare 1943
AQHA #2866

BARBRA B, by B'ar Hunter II out of a mare by Rainy Day, is holder of the World's Record for 300 yards and co-holder of the 440-yard record for 3-year-olds. Her fastest time of :22.4f was established when she won the Del Rio Sweepstakes (see Chart 605). Approximately four months later she won a match race from ***Fair Truckle** at Hollywood Park, Inglewood, California, in the fast time of :22.5f (see picture above). Out of a total of 10 races she won 8 and was second twice. On the opposite page are four of **BARBRA B's** stablemates, who are horses of outstanding racing ability. Our very capable trainer is Lyo Lee of Tucson, Arizona.

GILL CATTLE CO.   TUCSON, ARIZ.

ever seen. She was good to look at and good to be around."

By the time Barbra B was a 3-year-old, she was owned by Roy Gill of the Gill Cattle Company in Tucson, and she quickly established herself as a sizzling runner. According to the 1947 yearbook of the American Quarter Racing Association, "Barbra B won seven of her eight starts during the season (1946), defeating such horses as Vandy, Senor Bill, Flicka, Tonta Gal, Hard Twist, Pumpkin, Miss Bank, and *Fair Truckle (TB). She won the 3-Year-Old Championship at Albuquerque in 22.6 seconds, setting a world's record for 3-year-olds, and also won the Fall Championship Stakes for 3-Year-Olds at Rillito."

In May 1947, Barbra won a match race against Miss Bank at El Paso. The distance was 330 yards, and the bay mare set a track record. In a rematch a week or so later, Barbra B won once again, setting another track record, but all bets were called off because Miss Bank had injured herself coming out of the gate.

In August 1947, Barbra B caught the attention of racing fans all over the nation when she was matched against a Thoroughbred stallion, *Fair Truckle, at Holly-wood Park in Inglewood, California. In those days, match races were common, but not between a Quarter Horse and Thoroughbred, not on the hallowed grounds of a major Thoroughbred track, and not for the kind of money each owner put up: $50,000, winner take all.

The distance was a quarter-mile, the mare's best distance. One would think that a Thoroughbred would be at a disadvantage at this distance, but *Fair Truckle had some impressive fractional times for a quarter mile in his races. He was an Irish-bred stallion, owned by Charles S. Howard, trained by H. Philpot, and ridden by the legendary Johnny Longden. Barbra B, trained by Lyo Lee, was ridden by her regular jockey, Tony Licata.

Reports say that more than 5,000 people streamed into Hollywood Park, which had closed for the season, to see this extraordinary match race. The event had been advertised as closed to the public; otherwise, more people might have been on hand. There was no pari-mutuel wagering, but you can take it to the bank

Waggoner's Rainy Day appears in Barbra B's pedigree twice.

Ben Hur, the sire of Waggoner's Rainy Day.

the mare and did not interfere with her. Barbra B increased her lead, and when she crossed the wire about 2 lengths in front, jubilation reigned among the folks from cow country. The mare's time for the 440 yards was 22.5 seconds—taken by four watches.

Later, untold thousands got to see the race when it was shown on the newsreel at many movie theaters. You could say that the newsreel was the forerunner of TV network news.

Ray Pinnel, who was a ranch manager for the Gill Cattle Company, in Oregon at the time, still remembers the race. "I sent money to California to be bet. I don't guess there's any way to prove it, but there was supposed to have been more than $1 million bet on the race. I do know they wanted to send an armored car to handle it."

Another old-timer says that Gill Ranch cowboys bet their saddles, spurs, bridles, etc., and just about broke the shedrow hands at Hollywood Park.

Later, Pinnel relocated to the company's California ranch, near Porterville, where he took care of Barbra B for several years. "She was a pretty bay mare," he recalls. "Gentle, sweet, and perfect to be around. Her foals were just like her. Some of her offspring were so good-natured we could put three kids on them at the same time. Barbra was kind, but she was also an individual with her own style. And she never had enough milk for her foals. We always had to use a goat."

The mare's official AQHA records reflect earnings of only $3,050, but keep in mind that she no doubt won a lot more money in unofficial match races.

Barbra B produced seven foals, none of whom did anything special on the track, although some had some success as breeding stock. They were: Barbara Tex, by My Texas Dandy Jr.; Pelican Gill, by Pelican; Barbara Grace, Captain Crusade, and Richie, all by Glass Truckle (TB); Adrienne, by Bar Tonto; and Joe B. Less, by Joe Less. Only Barbara Tex, Richie, and Joe B. Less earned an ROM in racing.

AQHA records list Henry F. Howison of Lemon Grove, Calif., as Barbra B's last owner. He acquired the mare in May 1964. Although no one seems to know when Barbra B died, she earned a permanent place in Quarter racing history.

that thousands of dollars changed hands in side bets.

*Fair Truckle broke from the gate first, but Barbra B took a substantial lead in the first 50 yards and continued to gain. As they approached the eighth pole, the stallion bore to the rail, but passed behind

CHICARO BILL

10

CHICARO BILL is not as well remembered today as some of the early Quarter Horse sires, but back in the 1930s, '40s, and even into the '50s, just about everybody in the Quarter Horse business knew who he was. And people in the racing game today still recognize his contribution to the industry.

Chicaro Bill not only sired some outstanding runners, but also went on to become a leading maternal grandsire of ROM race horses. Among his offspring was Chicado V, foaled in 1950 and out of the mare Do Good. Rated AAAT, Chicado V was the Champion Quarter Running 2-Year-Old in 1952. When retired for breeding, she produced Chicado Chick, AAA and an AQHA Champion; Three Chicks, AAAT and an AQHA Champion; Anchor Chic, Table Tennis, The Ole Man, and War Chic—all AAAT; and Successor, AA.

Another Chicaro Bill daughter was Flicka, who was rated AA on the track and produced Black Easter Bunny, Flicka Hyloah, and Kid Viersen, all rated AAA; and Flicka's Chick, AA.

The sons of Chicaro Bill were not the breeders that his daughters were, but one of the better known was Senor Bill. He earned a AAA rating on the track and

People in the racing game today still recognize his contribution to the industry.

Chicaro Bill, a good sire of performance horses and a terrific broodmare sire.

Photo Courtesy of AQHA

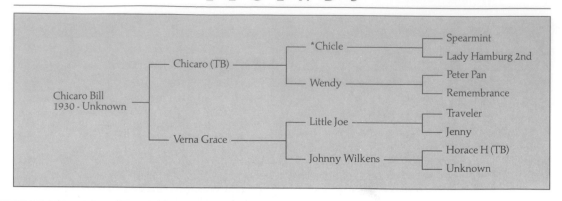

```
                                                                    ┌─── Spearmint
                                                    ┌─── *Chicle ────┤
                                   ┌─── Chicaro (TB)─┤                └─── Lady Hamburg 2nd
                                   │                 │                ┌─── Peter Pan
                                   │                 └─── Wendy ──────┤
 Chicaro Bill ─────────────────────┤                                  └─── Remembrance
 1930 - Unknown                    │                 ┌─── Little Joe ─┬─── Traveler
                                   │                 │                └─── Jenny
                                   └─── Verna Grace ─┤                ┌─── Horace H (TB)
                                                     └─── Johnny Wilkens ─┤
                                                                      └─── Unknown
```

Halter and Performance Record: None.

Progeny Record:

AQHA Champions: 0	Performance Points Earned: 2
Foal Crops: 21	Performance Registers of Merit: 1
Foals Registered: 180	Race Money Earned: $30,774
Halter-Point Earners: 4	Race Registers of Merit: 18
Halter Points Earned: 12	Race Starters: 31
Performance-Point Earners: 2	World Champions (Racing): 1
Leading Race Money Earner: Chicaro Deke ($8,093)	

Chicaro (TB), the sire of Chicaro Bill.

sired several ROM race and performance colts, and one AQHA Champion, Senora Michele.

Foaled in 1930, Chicaro Bill was bred by one of the noted horsemen of that era, John Dial of Goliad, Texas. Chicaro Bill's sire was Chicaro, a Thoroughbred by *Chicle, a leading sire in the late 1920s. *Chicle's sire, Spearmint, won the English Derby in 1906. It is believed that Chicaro (TB) never raced because of a foot injury. A heavily muscled Thoroughbred, Chicaro was used extensively in the Quarter Horse breeding program of the King Ranch.

Chicaro Bill's dam was Verna Grace, a daughter of Little Joe. At one point, Verna Grace was a registered Thoroughbred and went by the name of Fair Chance. In those days, of course, there was no AQHA, and it was not unusual for horses who were not straight Thoroughbred to be registered with The Jockey Club.

Verna Grace had speed bred into her through her sire, Little Joe, and maternal grandsire, Horace H (TB). But there are no records today indicating she ever raced.

Nor does Chicaro Bill have any official race record. However, John Almonds of Alice, Tex., remembers the horse. Almonds was a good friend and neighbor of Ott Adams, who owned Little Joe. "Although Chicaro Bill was a Quarter Horse," Almonds said, "John Dial used to race him as a Thoroughbred, which was easy to do in those days."

Almonds did not remember the specific circumstances, but said that Chicaro Bill injured a shoulder, and after that he could no longer race as a Thoroughbred because it was awkward for him to turn to the left.

Chicado V, one of Chicaro Bill's greatest daughters, and one of the greatest producers in AQHA history. Foaled in 1950, she was 3 years old when this picture was taken. She was owned by Frank Vessels for years.

Photo Courtesy of Vessels Stallion Farm

"After that," Almonds continued, "John Dial spent a lot of time trying to cook up a match race between Chicaro Bill and any takers. He wanted to match him on the straightaway as a Quarter Horse, but no one would take the challenge.

"In those days, most of us looked at Chicaro Bill as one of the best sires in the country. As far as we were concerned, many of those early Chicaro Bill mares were priceless."

At some point, John Dial sold Chicaro Bill to L.T. "Buster" Burns of Yoakum, Tex., according to Almonds. "Burns later sold the horse to Ronald Mason, Nowata, Oklahoma." Mason's Cross J Ranch, where Oklahoma Star also stood, was at that time a leading producer of race and roping horses—and Chicaro Bill sired some terrific rope horses.

Continuing, Almonds said, "From Mason's ranch, Chicaro Bill was sold to Elmer Hepler in New Mexico. Then I lost track of him." The stallion's last home was with Glenn Chipperfield of Phoenix, who registered him with the AQHA.

Almonds, who bred several of his own mares to Chicaro Bill, describes the horse as "one of the most powerful I've ever

Chicado V winning an October '53 race at the Los Angeles County Fair, with jockey Jack Brown. That's Robin Reed placing second, and Miss Cinders, third. **Photo Courtesy of Vessels Stallion Farm**

A 1953 winner's circle photo of Chicado V, with jockey Jack Brown.
Photo Courtesy of Vessels Stallion Farm

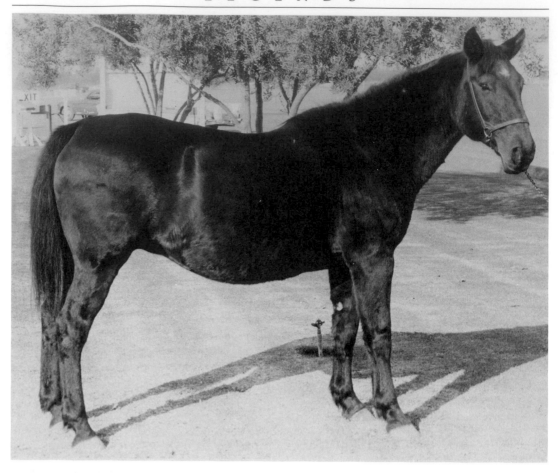

Do Good, the dam of Chicado V, was foaled in 1938 and was sired by a horse called St. Louis. She also produced Senor Bill, Clabber II (by Clabber), and six other ROM race colts.

Photo Courtesy of Vessels Stallion Farm

Senor Bill, one of the best sons of Chicaro Bill.
Photo by Richard Schaus, Courtesy of Phil Livingston

seen. He must have weighed over 1,300 pounds and stood 16 hands. But despite his size, he moved light as a cat."

Chicaro Bill was either a bay or brown with three white feet and a blaze. Almonds continues, "One of the peculiar things about him was that many foals from his first crops carried a lot of white, but foals from his later crops had less and less white."

Someone else who remembers Chicaro Bill is Arizonan Franklin Cox. He says the horse "had a good disposition, and his offspring were the same way. I ran both Senor Bill and Settle Up (a grandson of Chicaro Bill) at Rillito. Senor Bill held a world record for stallions for several years. That was back when we raced our horses, and then turned around and roped off them."

The 1947 yearbook of the American Quarter Racing Association had this to say about Senor Bill:

"Senor Bill, 1943 brown horse, by Chicaro Bill and out of Do Good, by St. Louis, started 16 times during the season.

A very fast but also very erratic horse, he won three of his starts, finished second five times, third three times, and was unplaced five times. At El Paso in the fall, he set a track record for 330 yards; ran second to Miss Bank in the Sheriff's Posse Stakes . . . and then went on to Rillito to defeat Miss Bank by a head at the same distance (350 yards).

"He did not win again until the 1947 Speed Trials at Rillito when he defeated Prissy, Hank H, and others in the 330-yard Speed Stakes in 17.4 seconds and equaled the world record for that distance. Senor Bill is a very compact horse of excellent conformation who should sire good cow horses as well as Quarter running horses."

In talking about Chicaro Bill, Franklin Cox says, "Glenn Chipperfield got a lot of mares to Chicaro Bill. There were a few who came from California and New Mexico, but most were from Arizona."

Buck Nichols of Gilbert, Ariz., says this about Chicaro Bill. "Glenn was retired when he bought Chicaro Bill. He was an older horse by then, fat and out of shape, but still good-looking with an excellent disposition. We had a lot of great horses in our part of the country, and Chicaro Bill was definitely one of them."

Veteran horseman Tom Finley of Gilbert, Ariz., remembers Chicaro Bill "as a big, stout horse. In his day, mutton withers were sort of popular, but he was a more upstanding type, smooth-built. He showed his Thoroughbred blood, but he was also heavy-muscled.

"In my opinion, his most outstanding offspring in these parts was Senor Bill, who raced as well as showed. I had a nice filly by him who won her first start and several races after that. There's no doubt that Chicaro Bill was an outstanding individual."

It's not known for sure when Chicaro Bill died, but his death came as a result of unusual circumstances. Evidently he had

Settle Up, by Parker's Chicaro and a grandson of Chicaro Bill, was AA on the track, a grand champion at halter many times, and a good rope horse. He's shown here with owner Franklin Cox after being named grand champion stallion at an Arizona show, probably in the late '40s or early '50s. Settle Up also sired a number of foals who earned their ROMs on the track or in the arena. **Photo by Richard Schaus**

contracted a case of mange, which Chipperfield was treating. In trying to scratch his itchy places, the horse rubbed against some oleanders—plants that are very toxic to livestock. Apparently toxins from the oleanders caused complications with the mange, resulting in his death.

Despite his size, he moved light as a cat.

11 QUEENIE

She was by the renowned Flying Bob, one of the greatest sires of racing Quarter Horses.

THERE WAS a time in racing history when anyone feeling the urge to brag on the speed of his horse opened his wallet. In those days, the 1930s and 1940s and even farther back, bragging meant betting. If you didn't have enough hard cash to secure your wager, you could always ante up with land, a house, a horse, a flock of chickens, or maybe your best hunting dog. Sometimes entire towns—as in the case of McKinney, Tex., in 1856 when Steel Dust matched Monmouth—could

end up on the verge of bankruptcy.

There were certain names that reigned supreme in the '20s, '30s, and '40s. They were names such as Miss Princess (Woven Web), Clabber, Queenie, Shue Fly, Joe Reed, Miss Bank, Hard Twist, and Cowboy.

"There were so many great horses back then," says Frances Jelks, widow of the late Rukin Jelks, whose name was associated with such notable individuals as Rukin String and Old Pueblo (TB). "And racing was different, too," she continued. "It was

Queenie, one of the greatest Quarter racing mares in history. When this photo was taken, she was owned by Rukin Jelks.

Photo Courtesy of Phil Livingston

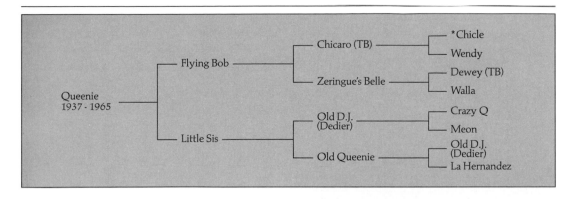

Queenie 1937 - 1965
- Flying Bob
  - Chicaro (TB)
    - *Chicle
    - Wendy
  - Zeringue's Belle
    - Dewey (TB)
    - Walla
- Little Sis
  - Old D.J. (Dedier)
    - Crazy Q
    - Meon
  - Old Queenie
    - Old D.J. (Dedier)
    - La Hernandez

really sporting fun. We bragged on our horses and then we matched them. The good ones always met up with one another more than once."

Some of the greatest emerged from Louisiana, a hot bed of short racing in the 1920s and '30s. It was the bayou country that took credit for the likes of Lightfoot Sis (dam of Go Man Go), Dedier (Old D.J.), Della Moore, and Queenie.

It was 1937 when Queenie took her first gulp of Cajun air at Martin Richard's farm in Rayne, Louisiana. Her pedigree evidenced some of the state's finest bloodlines. She was by the renowned Flying Bob, one of the greatest sires of racing Quarter Horses in the 1930s and '40s. In his book *Quarter Horses: A Story of Two Centuries*, Bob Denhardt wrote:

"Flying Bob was unbeatable (as a sire) when crossed on Louisiana mares sired by Old D.J., as the great Louisiana short-horse stallion Dedier was commonly called. It was D.J. who put the Louisiana Cajuns into the horse business in the early 1900s. Later, when his fillies were crossed to Flying Bob, a whole family of short horses was created that rocked Texas and the Southwest. It was necessary for Texans to go to Louisiana and buy Flying Bobs to stay in the race horse business."

Flying Bob was by Chicaro (TB), and out of Zeringue's Belle, sometimes referred to as Belle Z. She was by Dewey (TB), and out of a War Eagle mare named Walla, and was the pride and joy of Noah Zeringue of Erath, Louisiana. Belle was one tough race horse, and her match winnings contributed to the support of Zeringue and his family for a number of years. After her reputation spread so far that Zeringue could no longer drum up match

races for her, he bred her to Chicaro. And he named the resulting colt Bob, after Chicaro's owner, Bob Carter.

Zeringue initially registered Bob as a Thoroughbred. The secret was well kept until the stallion began distinguishing himself in race after race at shorter distances. When it was learned that Bob wasn't a

Halter and Performance Record: Racing Register of Merit; World Champion Quarter Running Mare: 1944-45, 1945-46; World Champion Quarter Running Horse: 1945-46.

Produce of Dam Record:

Little Queeny	1948 mare by Piggin String (TB) Racing Register of Merit
Queen O' Clubs J	1949 mare by Piggin String (TB) Racing Register of Merit
Rukin String	1950 stallion by Piggin String (TB) Racing Register of Merit 1953 World Champion Quarter Running Stallion
Gunny Sack	1951 gelding by Piggin String (TB) Racing Register of Merit
Joe Queen	1952 stallion by Joe Reed II Racing Register of Merit
Edam Tailor	1953 stallion by Tailor Made C
Queenie's Girl	1954 mare by Tailor Made C
Bond Issue	1955 stallion by Bymeabond (TB) Racing Register of Merit
Alliance	1956 stallion by Alumnus (TB) Racing Register of Merit
Miss Queenie	1958 mare by Depth Charge (TB) Racing Register of Merit

Flying Bob, the sire of Queenie.

Photo Courtesy of Phil Livingston

One of Queenie's best sons was Joe Queen, who was featured on the February '58 WH cover with his owner, Audie Murphy, a World War II hero who went on to fame in Hollywood.

Thoroughbred, Zeringue changed the stallion's name to Flying Bob. Besides, adding the "Flying" seemed especially appropriate, since more than one person who watched the stallion run said he could literally fly.

Zeringue was an enterprising individual. He figured he had something special in Flying Bob. After all, he was by Chicaro, one of the finest stallions of the period. He was out of Belle Z and, as far as Zeringue was concerned, mares didn't come any better than her. In Zeringue's mind, a plan emerged that resulted in one of the first horse trailers in Louisiana. Zeringue built it himself, and immediately loaded Flying Bob. His destination and objective? He offered a traveling stud service.

Zeringue was extremely particular when it came to the mares for Flying Bob. He wanted only the best. He had supreme confidence in his stallion, but at the same time, he believed firmly that the dam contributes 70 percent to the foal. Queenie's dam, one of the chosen mares, was owned by Martin Richard. She was a good mare, but there is confusion about her breeding, as well as her name. In AQHA's Studbook No. 3, Queenie's dam is listed as Sis, by Doc Horn (TB), and the dam of Sis is listed

"DEE DEE"
A.Q.H.A.# 2512
SIRE: FLYING BOB...DAM: EMERGENCY
1945 WORLD CHAMPION QUARTER RUNNING STALLION

Dee Dee, World Champion Quarter Running Stallion in 1944-45, was a half-brother to Queenie, as his sire was also Flying Bob. Although this photo lists Dee Dee's dam as Emergency, AQHA records state that Dee Dee was out of Sis, by Doc Horn (TB).

Photo Courtesy of Phil Livingston

The bay filly hit the tracks and left a blazing trail of Cajun fire behind her.

as Old Queenie, by Old D.J., whose real name was Dedier. As the story goes, horsemen began calling him Old D.J. because they found Dedier difficult to pronounce.

Regardless, AQHA records now state that the dam of Queenie was Little Sis, by Old D.J. Old Queenie is still recognized as the dam of Little Sis, but now AQHA says that the sire and dam of Old Queenie are Old D.J. and La Hernandez. It's another one of those situations that will never be resolved, and today, it doesn't matter.

What is significant is that Little Sis, when bred to Flying Bob, produced a filly who would become a legend.

Richard was pleased when Queenie was born. She was a fine-looking little filly, and Richard figured he could either sell her or race her. But when he made a trip to Queenie's pasture early one morning, he found her with a pronounced limp in her right front foot. Nothing seemed to help the situation

and, before too long, her hoof began deteriorating. The result was a deformed foot, referred to as a club foot. Richard felt fortunate when George Orr of El Paso, Tex., said he'd like to buy the crippled filly.

Over the years, the story revolving around Queenie and her foot has changed back and forth. Some people insist it was a genetic deformity. Still others say it was a babyhood injury that wasn't treated properly. Regardless, it didn't stop Queenie from running. The bay filly hit the tracks and left a blazing trail of Cajun fire behind her. She ran on guts, heart, and raw courage.

At maturity, Queenie stood approximately 15 hands and weighed 1,000 pounds. In anybody's estimation, she was a compact package of running fury. In 1944, the crippled bay mare beat the immortal Shue Fly at the New Mexico

85

State Fair. Also in the stellar lineup were Squaw H and Piggin String (TB). The distance was 440 yards. Queenie barreled out of the gate and, halfway down the straightaway, the shoe flew off her club foot. She didn't stop. She didn't even slow down, and crossed the finish line in 21.4 seconds for a track record. There was $1,700 bet on the side, and it went home in Orr's pocket.

Queenie's most outstanding offspring included Rukin String.

"That's when Rukin told George (Orr) he wanted first shot at buying Queenie if he ever decided to sell her," said Frances Jelks. "Rukin finally got his chance. She was already a champion when we bought her, but she went on to set another record."

Queenie beat Miss Bank, another of the early stars, going 440 yards under 127 pounds in 22.5. Before she retired, Queenie was named World Champion Quarter Running Mare in 1944-45 and 1945-46, and World Champion Quarter Running Horse in 1945-46.

"I know her foot must have been extremely painful," recalled Frances Jelks. "There were times when it would crack open and bleed during a race. Rukin retired her in '46 and began breeding her. One of her more outstanding offspring was Rukin String, by Piggin String (TB).

"You certainly couldn't say Queenie was a pretty mare. She was a dark bay, heavy quartered, and muscular. And she most definitely had a mind of her own. You couldn't refer to her as mean because she wasn't, but she absolutely was not feminine. Maybe life was just too tough for her to be feminine."

As a producer, Queenie's most outstanding offspring were Rukin String, who earned three champion racing titles before distinguishing himself as an excellent sire; and Joe Queen, by Joe Reed II, who was a record-holder at 220 yards and became a noteworthy sire.

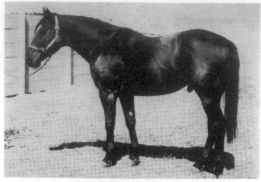

Piggin String (TB), the sire of several of Queenie's good foals.

Rukin and Frances Jelks eventually sold Queenie. Ultimately, the mare wound up with Art Pollard, who once owned a band of broodmares that included Queenie, Miss Bank, Miss Panama, and Hula Girl, and stallions such as Spotted Bull (TB) and Lightning Bar.

"Rukin sold Queenie to Bert Wood (owner of Joe Reed II), and Bert sold her to Audie Murphy. I bought her from Audie," recounted Pollard, who now lives in Washington state. She was 19 or 20 when I got her.

"She was a little mare. I think her heart must have been the biggest thing about her. Every time she ran, the shoe on that bad foot would come off and the foot would bleed. You know that must have hurt like hell."

Queenie was supposed to be in foal when Pollard bought her, but as things turned out, she wasn't. Pollard was disappointed, but he elected to keep the great old mare.

"I kept her in a soft pen so her foot wouldn't bother her," he mused. "She grazed and had access to all the feed she could eat. I was proud to have her, and I'm proud to know she's buried on my old ranch in Arizona." Pollard can't remember for sure when the mare died, but believes it was 1965.

There are still a few old-timers around who remember the streak of Cajun fire Queenie laid down every time she roared from a starting gate. And they still respect and admire the little mare with the big heart and club foot.

JOE HANCOCK 12

TOM HANCOCK of Nocona, Tex., isn't referring to Indians when he says he's "the last of the Mohicans."

In Hancock terminology, that phrase means Tom is the last of the Hancock clan to be directly associated with the famed horse named Joe Hancock.

The first order of business in a Hancock narrative is to put into perspective a few genealogical facts. In so doing, it's important to keep in mind the double names—like Billy Bob—so prevalent in Texas. John Jackson Hancock lived in Indian Territory approximately a stone's throw from Spanish Fort. Credited as the breeder of Joe Hancock, he was noted for raising fast horses in the late 1800s. His dominant bloodlines were what the later and more organized Quarter Horse folks would refer to as Steeldusts and Copperbottoms.

John Jackson eventually moved from the Spanish Fort area and homesteaded approximately 20 miles south of Perryton in the

He was one of the all-time great sires of rope horses.

Joe Hancock, circa 1927.

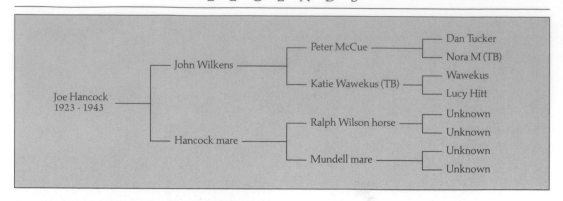

			Dan Tucker
		Peter McCue	Nora M (TB)
	John Wilkens	Katie Wawekus (TB)	Wawekus
Joe Hancock			Lucy Hitt
1923 - 1943		Ralph Wilson horse	Unknown
			Unknown
	Hancock mare	Mundell mare	Unknown
			Unknown

Halter and Performance Record: None.

Progeny Record:

Foal Crops: 15
Foals Registered: 155
Performance-Point Earners: 2
Performance Points Earned: 23
Leading Race Money Earner: Wonder Lad ($337)

Race Money Earned: $337
Race Registers of Merit: 6
Race Starters: 7

Joe David Hancock grew up with horses and nurtured what was to become an abiding love of racing.

rugged Texas panhandle. He ran a band of 35 to 40 broodmares with a roan stallion he called Old Deck, a son of Little Danger and, possibly, a grandson of Cold Deck.

Numbered among John Jackson's broodmares was a "breedy-type mare of Steeldust" lineage. Her conformation hinted at Thoroughbred blood, and John Jackson referred to her as the Mundell mare. The name seemed appropriate since he purchased her from a "traveling race horse man" named Mundell. It was this same mare who was destined to become the maternal granddam of Joe Hancock.

In 1885, John Jackson Hancock gave the name of Joe David to one of his sons. Joe David grew up with horses and nurtured what was to become an abiding love of racing. When he married, it was to a woman named Cora from the family known as Keck. The alliance was a strong one since Keck is another name to be reckoned with in the annals of running horse history. Included among the family is Newt Keck, who has trained three winners of the lucrative All-American Futurity. It was Joe

David who would eventually become responsible for raising and racing Joe Hancock.

In 1930, Joe David and Cora christened one of their sons Tom Hancock. Tom and his wife, Rita, reside in the nearly 100-year-old farmhouse at Nocona. Tom can still point to the pasture where Joe Hancock the horse roamed with mares when he wasn't lapping and tapping at match races. Tom never saw the part-Percheron stallion race, but he did grow up with the stories surrounding him. He's preserved old photographs, and he made notes and chronicled as much as he could about Joe Hancock before all those associated with him passed away. That, then, is why the story of Joe Hancock is best told by Tom.

"I'm not absolutely certain when Joe Hancock was foaled," began Tom. "Some records say 1923. Others say 1925.

"Whichever, I don't suppose it's critical. A lot of reports about Joe Hancock don't make much of the bottom side of his pedigree. His dam was a Hancock mare who was out of the Mundell mare. This Mundell mare had a colt by Old Deck while Granddaddy was still living in the Indian Territory. He named the colt Jeff."

Jeff grew up to become one fast race horse who was never beaten.

"My daddy, as well as my uncles, used to say that on a perfectly calm day Jeff could run 200 or 300 yards so fast he'd bring tears to the rider's eyes. The real point of all this is that the bottom of Joe's pedigree produced speed."

Most accounts of Joe Hancock describe him as a big horse who stood a solid 16 hands. That, however, is not the way Tom remembers the stallion. "He stood 15.2 or

Joe Hancock in the trailer in which he was hauled from the Texas panhandle to Nocona. The fellow tying the rope is the two-legged Joe Hancock.

maybe 15.3," he attested, "but certainly not 16. He was dark brown with that white blaze running down his face. That much I do remember."

John Wilkens, the sire of Joe Hancock, was a legend in his own right. John Jackson Hancock, always appreciative of good horseflesh, bought John Wilkens from the old JA Ranch when the stallion was 15 years old. With John Wilkens in hand, why did John Jackson elect to breed his Mundell mare to a Percheron stallion and thus produce the Hancock mare that would become Joe Hancock's dam?

"No one really knew why," Tom commented. "Two of Granddaddy's neighbors were bachelor brothers named Ralph and Dave Wilson. Ralph owned a registered, little-boned Percheron. Daddy said he was a black horse that stood about 14.3 hands and weighed around 1,100 pounds. He wasn't a draft-horse type, which is what most people think of when they hear the word Percheron. He was Ralph Wilson's personal saddle horse. As the story goes, Ralph Wilson would ride that Percheron to town or to gather cattle, or he'd run you a race on him.

"Granddaddy Hancock bred five or six of his mares to the Percheron. Why did he do it? Well, the reasons were known only to him, and he never told anyone else what they were! Among the ones bred to the Percheron was the Mundell mare. The following year, she produced a brown filly who would become the mama of Joe Hancock. No one called her anything other than the Hancock mare.

"Now, don't forget that the Mundell mare had produced Jeff. And Daddy and his brothers used to say Jeff was the only horse they thought might have been able to outrun Joe Hancock. It was this Mundell mare who, when bred to the Percheron, produced the Hancock mare who produced Joe Hancock. Based on all this, I think it's safe to say Joe Hancock didn't get all his speed and potency from John Wilkens, who was a son of Peter McCue."

Tom Hancock is adamant when it comes to attributing at least a fair share of credit to Joe Hancock's bottom side pedigree. As testimonial, he relates a conversation he once overheard between his daddy (Joe

The two Joe Hancocks at the family home in Nocona.

Hancock) and Uncle Bird Ogle, the trainer who brought Joe Hancock to racing fame.

"I heard them talking," remarks Tom, "and they agreed that quite possibly Old Joe did, in fact, receive a number of positive benefits from that Percheron stallion. They listed those benefits as his strength in stature, his bone, his appetite (he was known to eat all his bedding on more than one occasion), his outstanding

calmness and disposition, and his speed.

"Daddy and Uncle Bird agreed on another quality about Joe . . . his conformation. They used to say they couldn't improve on it for racing even if they could take a pencil and literally redraw it.

"I don't think the Hancock speed was ever a point of controversy, but I can't say the same about his conformation. As a matter of fact, his conformation took quite a beating in later years when he was an aged horse, being pasture-bred.

"Regardless of what anyone may have said about Joe Hancock, there were some noted horsemen in whose opinion he was outstanding. Elmer Hepler often said he was one of the best-looking horses he'd ever seen. Tom Burnett of the 6666/Triangle Ranch was also quoted as saying Joe was one of the most outstanding-looking horses he'd ever looked at. Newt Keck, who saw Joe when he was a 2- and 3-year-old, always insisted Joe could go to the track today and not be out of place in terms of conformation. He said he looked good then and he'd still look good today. He further said Joe had the best hip and one of the heaviest loins he'd ever seen on a horse. My mother, Cora Hancock, always said Joe was not only good-looking but a perfect gentleman as well."

Since Joe Hancock was bred by John Jackson Hancock in the Texas panhandle, how did the stallion make his way into the hands of Joe David Hancock? "Perryton was about 300 miles away," explained Tom, "and each summer the family met there for a reunion.

"The family began gathering one summer, and my daddy and his cousin, Walter Allred, went out to the pasture to get a couple of horses to ride. They found a colt with a wire cut on his shoulder. They told Granddaddy about the colt, who didn't have a name. They brought him up, and Daddy started doctoring on him.

"Daddy and Granddaddy also discovered that the brown colt, a yearling at the time, was still nursing his mama. They decided to keep him up and wean him. It was a 300-mile trip by dirt road between Daddy's house in Nocona and Granddaddy's place in the panhandle, so Daddy decided to stay a couple of weeks. He kept working with the brown colt, doctoring him, and halter-breaking him.

"I think Daddy must have started trying to figure out how to keep the colt as soon as he saw him, and he finally managed to trade Granddaddy for him. The next problem was getting him from Perryton to Nocona. Daddy finally borrowed a wooden, open trailer from Dave Wilson. They loaded the brown colt and started the 2-day trip home."

With the brown colt safely corralled at the Hancock farm, Joe David dismantled the slat-sided trailer and shipped it by train back to Dave Wilson.

"Daddy turned Joe out in a pasture," continued Tom. "He later found out the colt had gotten a mare in foal. The result of that fortunate accident was a filly who was the image of Joe himself. She wasn't as big, but everything else was the same. None of us knew it at the time, but that filly was to become the foundation mare for all Daddy's horses as well as mine. We called her Winnie Mae but, in later years, her registered name became Jose Wilkens. One thing for sure . . . she was extremely fast.

"One day, Daddy had Joe positioned in a cutting harness, getting him ready for the vet to geld. The vet arrived and so did a friend of Daddy's named Tom Skinner. Both men looked at Joe and Tom remarked: 'Damn, Joe, I wouldn't geld this colt.'

"I guess everybody owes a debt to Mr. Skinner for giving Daddy that piece of advice. It wasn't that Daddy didn't think Joe was good enough to keep as a stallion. He did, but he just wasn't into having stallions at the farm.

"My daddy and oldest brother, Jack, broke Joe Hancock as a 2-year-old. It wasn't long before they discovered what they'd always suspected to be true—that he had a world of speed. They ran him two or three times around Nocona and Spanish Fort, and he showed his heels to everyone. Daddy was convinced the colt could run. That's when he made the decision to take him to a trainer named Elbert Bird Ogle. At that time, Uncle Bird, as we called him, was a renowned trainer of race horses. He lived in Claypool,

Tom Hancock remembers all of the stories about old Joe Hancock.

Okla., so Daddy got on a saddle horse and led Joe across the Red River to Claypool.

"Payment for training back in those days—in the mid-1920s—was simple. Daddy paid Uncle Bird one dollar a day and furnished the feed.

"The first race Uncle Bird put Joe in was at Comanche, Oklahoma. He walked up to make the entry, and the man writing down the information asked for the colt's name. Well, the colt didn't have a name. Uncle Bird commented he was owned by Joe Hancock at Nocona, so just call him Joe Hancock."

So it was that the brown colt officially became Joe Hancock; and that's when he began establishing a racing legacy. Those were the days of great match racing. It was lap and tap or line starts on dirt roads. In some ways, those were the true glory days of racing.

"Daddy only saw Joe Hancock run three times," mused Tom. "Daddy wasn't a racetracker. He stayed home, farmed, raised six kids, and other good horses.

"Uncle Bird ran Joe during the summer and brought him back to Daddy in the winter. Joe bred a few mares while he was home. All this was back when horses were everything. Granddaddy and Daddy both

Those were the days of great match racing.

Joe Hancock winning a race at Pawhuska, Okla., with Hack Winters in the irons.

"Before his career was over, Joe was open to the world at any distance from the starting line to three-eighths of a mile."

knew good race horses; but they also worked them, cowboyed on them, and played on them. Daddy never bred a mare hoping to get just a good working horse, and neither did Granddaddy. They wanted speed because, back then, speed was a main factor.

"Before his career was over, Joe was open to the world at any distance from the starting line to three-eighths of a mile. I never heard of a horse who beat him at the quarter, but there was one by old Chester B. who beat him one time at a half-mile. Other than that, Joe always won his half-mile races. A lot of times he did it by being so fast away from the line that the other horse couldn't catch him.

"I have no idea how many times Joe ran,

or how much money he earned for his supporters. I know he bought some farms for people. There was one banker from Oklahoma who was a hard gambler, and he backed Joe with a lot of dollars.

"There was a mare by the name of Red Nell that Joe was matched with twice. The first time was in Oklahoma City just after a little rain shower. George Ogle, Uncle Bird's son, was on Joe. Don't forget, there were no gates back then, and Joe had a way of walking up to the starting line and then squirming. That's what he did when George brought him against Red Nell the first time.

"Joe twisted around at the line until his front feet were nearly crossed. Well, the starter was watching heads, not feet. He turned them loose, and Red Nell got off in front because Joe had to uncross his feet before he could move.

"Red Nell came from south Texas. She was a short horse whose best distance was 220 yards. She stood pat (meaning she'd take on any challenger) at either 250 or 350. I can't remember which one at this point.

"Anyway, Joe finally uncrossed his legs and took off. George Ogle didn't realize what had happened, and couldn't figure out why Joe was late leaving. George had a lot of money on the line, so he started playing Yankee Doodle on Joe's rear end. Nothing seemed to help. Joe just wasn't gaining on that mare. Finally, George realized the ground was just wet enough to make Joe slip. He threw away his stick, wrapped up, and started talking to ol' Joe, who started gaining. They hit dry ground just before the finish, and Joe got by Red Nell.

"Well, that race was over but the story wasn't. Red Nell's people hadn't seen Joe's crossed legs at the start of the race. They made a rematch right then and there at one-eighth of a mile. This time, Joe out-broke the mare and beat her bad. My cousin, Joe, was there to see the whole thing."

It was nearly impossible for Joe Hancock to find any takers by the time he was standing pat at three-eighths of a mile. That, however, didn't mean George and Bird Ogle quit trying.

"Oh, no," laughed Tom. "Back when Arlington Downs was still open in Dallas, George took his Thoroughbreds there along with Joe, and told everybody Joe was his pony horse. W.T. Waggoner—the famous Waggoner with all the horses—owned Arlington Downs and had his stable right on the grounds. What George really wanted was to run Joe against one of Waggoner's own horses, but he was trying to figure out how to do it without revealing Joe's identity.

"One day a group of guys was talking, and included in the bunch was one of Waggoner's main men. George remarked he had a pony horse at the barn he'd be willing to match against any taker. But the real identity of George's 'pony horse' got to Waggoner, who, in turn, said to his man: 'You mean I have a million dollars worth of

This picture of Joe Hancock appeared in Vol. 1, No. 1 of the AQHA Studbook, when Joe was owned by the Tom L. Burnett Estate.
Photo Courtesy of AQHA

horses out here and nothing to outrun his pony horse?' His man told him he was correct. Waggoner wouldn't match."

There finally came a time when Joe Hancock simply ran out of competition. He stood pat at three-eighths of a mile, but no one wanted to take on the brown stallion. He'd run for a good half-dozen years, and it looked as if it might be time for his life to take another direction.

"I can remember Daddy telling the story about the day George Ogle came to our house in Nocona," chuckled Tom. His purpose was to buy Joe Hancock. They visited and visited and dinner time came. They ate and visited some more. George was still there when supper time was coming around.

"Finally, Daddy thought to himself he'd get rid of George if he'd just price the horse so high George would give up and leave. Don't forget, these were the Depression days. So, Daddy said, 'Alright,

Red Man, one of Joe Hancock's greatest sons, was a terrific sire of rope and race horses. He was bred by the Burnett Ranches, and was out of a Burnett Ranch mare. Because of his ears, which were frozen off when he was a foal, Red Man was sometimes referred to as the "the Cyrano de Bergerac of horses." He was owned for much of his life by Kenny Gunter of Benson, Arizona. **Photo Courtesy of Phil Livingston**

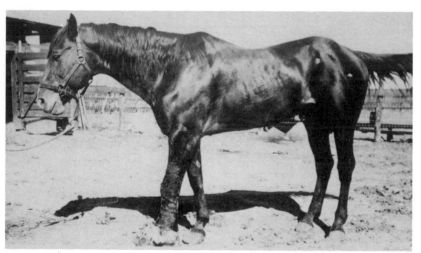

This photo was taken of Joe after he cut his left front foot, and about a year before he had to be put down.

give me $1,000.' That was certainly a lot of money then, but George didn't lose a breath in accepting the price. He paid Daddy right there and picked up ol' Joe within the next 2 days. He delivered him to Tom Burnett at Iowa Park, Texas. What did Mr. Burnett pay George for Joe Hancock? $2,000!

"Joe lived out his days with Burnett at the 6666/Triangle Ranches. Joe was out in the pasture when he cut his foot on wire. A bad infection set in, and the foot was a mess by the time Joe was found and taken to Dr. Smith in Abilene.

"Dr. Smith gave Joe total attention. He brought him out of the problem, but then Joe foundered about a year later. He was put down July 29, 1943. He was 20 years old, provided the 1923 foaling date is correct."

Joe David and Cora Hancock are buried in the Nocona cemetery. At the head of the double grave is a granite marker. Over Cora's name is her picture. Over Joe David's name is a picture of himself holding the reins of Joe Hancock.

Many ropers of today say that Joe Hancock was the all-time greatest sire of rope horses. Even third- and fourth-generation Hancocks have made good rope horses. Back in the 1950s, Shoat Webster of Lenapah, Okla., won a number of steer roping championships on a horse called Popcorn, a 1,200-pound gelding of Hancock breeding. Another great steer roper of that era was Everett Shaw of Stonewall, Oklahoma. He roped on Peanuts, who was by Roan Hancock by Joe Hancock. Peanuts and Popcorn are but two of old Joe's descendants who gained fame in the roping world.

Old-time ropers say that the Hancocks were big, stout, and tough, with lots of bone. Some of the geldings were also said to be snorty, with a few prone to buck, but they weren't bad. Possibly it was related to how they were handled. Most of the Hancocks were brown, dark bay, or roan. Many had big feet, and big heads that certainly could not be called pretty. Most of them had good withers, cinched deep, and sure-enough could run. Quite a few made their way to the race track, as well as the rodeo arena. Because they were so durable, the Hancocks could stand up under a lot of hauling.

Many of today's Hancock-bred horses still have the typical Hancock conformation, even after all these years. And ropers still swear by these big, plain-headed, but hard-working horses.

Joe Hancock is indeed a legend, and in 1992 he received recognition for his contribution to the Quarter Horse industry when he was inducted into the AQHA Hall of Fame.

COWBOY P-12

WHO WAS Cowboy P-12? When was he foaled? Who was his sire? Who owned him and bred him? Controversy surrounds all those questions. Everyone offers a different answer, a different perspective, a different set of facts and recollections. Amid all the divergence, however, there is one common denominator. Specifically, almost everyone agrees Cowboy was one of the finest horses who ever lived. They maintain that opinion regardless of whether the horse is discussed as a sire, as a runner, or as a solid using horse.

As is true with a number of other horses foaled in the 1920s and '30s, there is no way to verify the basic information about Cowboy. For example, AQHA's Vol. 1 No. 3 *Stud Book* states that Cowboy was foaled in 1922, bred by W. T. Waggoner of Electra, Tex., and owned by Cliff Fahrion, Bayfield, Colorado. His sire was listed as Buck Thomas, by Peter McCue, and his dam as a Yellow Wolf mare.

But in the "Errata" section of the No. 4

Cowboy was one of the finest horses who ever lived.

Clifford Fahrion and Cowboy in 1943.

Photo Courtesy of Howard Fahrion

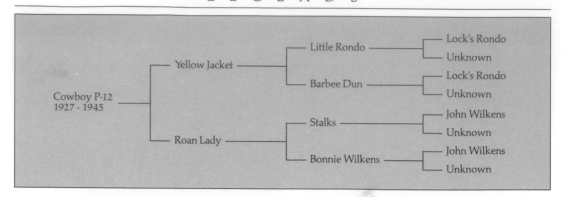

Cowboy P-12
1927 - 1945

Yellow Jacket
- Little Rondo
  - Lock's Rondo
  - Unknown
- Barbee Dun
  - Lock's Rondo
  - Unknown

Roan Lady
- Stalks
  - John Wilkens
  - Unknown
- Bonnie Wilkens
  - John Wilkens
  - Unknown

Halter and Performance Record: None.

Progeny Record:

Foal Crops: 16	Performance Points Earned: 1
Foals Registered: 130	Race Money Earned: $14,410
Halter-Point Earners: 6	Race Registers of Merit: 10
Halter Points Earned: 11	Race Starters: 17
Performance-Point Earners: 1	World Champions (Racing): 2
Leading Race Money Earner: Hard Twist ($6,319)	

"His sire, Yellow Jacket, was the most celebrated running Quarter Horse in the whole Southwest."

Stud Book, a correction for Cowboy states that he was foaled in 1927 and was bred by Edgar Thompson of Stinnett, Texas. His sire was listed as Yellow Jacket by Little Rondo. There are even some folks who insist Cowboy was an own son of Peter McCue.

We will never know which breeding is correct, but the fact that Cowboy was a heck of a good horse is what's important. In the April '51 issue of *Western Horseman*, in an article about Hard Twist, Nelson C. Nye wrote:

"Hard Twist's sire, Cowboy P-12, has been justly celebrated as one of the greatest cattle working horses in the country. Cowboy was out of one of the greatest mares in the Panhandle, Roan Lady, by Stalks. His sire, Yellow Jacket, was the most celebrated running Quarter Horse in the whole South-

west until Possum beat him at Kyle, Tex., very nearly throwing the town into the hands of the receivers. Cowboy sired 10 horses that got their AQHA Register of Merit, including Shue Fly, Gangster D., LaChee, Bulldog, Mug, Georgie F., and Basin Bess, as well as Hard Twist."

Jim Norton of Bayfield, in southwest Colorado, had the good fortune of knowing Cowboy when the horse was owned by Cliff Fahrion and Sandy Scott. He was also lucky enough to own several outstanding Cowboy progeny.

"I owned Bulldog and Bay Betty, plus Pakeeta and Peggy Ann," Norton says. "Pakeeta was the granddam of Tonteeta, who set a world record for me at 250 yards at La Mesa Park in 1965. The time was rejected by AQHA, though, because she carried 114 pounds and the base weight for a world record for 3-year-old fillies was 116 pounds.

"Bulldog set a track record at 550 yards at Rillito Park in Tucson in 1945. Shue Fly set a 440-yard world record in 22.3 seconds. That, I believe, was in 1942. Hard Twist was the AQHA Champion Quarter Running Stallion in 1946, 1947, and 1951, and both he and Bulldog were foals of 1942.

"The mares I owned by Cowboy were Bay Betty, who was his last foal, and Peggy Ann, the granddam of three AAAT runners."

Sandy Scott, who now lives in Aztec, N.M., remembers Cowboy as "quite a horse . . . surely the best who ever came into our country." In the late 1930s, Scott and his

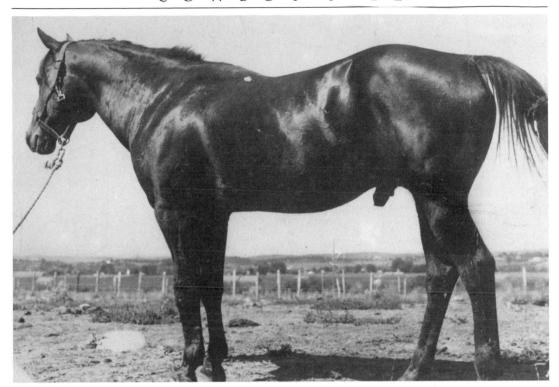

This photo of Cowboy P-12 was probably taken in the early 1940s.

Photo Courtesy of Howard Fahrion

dad, Pete, owned the Telawauket Dude Ranch about 18 miles from Bayfield, Colorado. They heard about Cowboy, who was owned by Ed Thompson of Blanco, N.M., less than 100 miles from Bayfield.

Sandy and Pete owned about 12 mares. Sandy relates, "When Dad got a good look at Cowboy, he said, 'We'd better get that horse.'" Thompson did not want to sell Cowboy, so the Scotts borrowed him and took him to Bayfield. "We bred our mares and some outside mares," Sandy says.

He adds, "Later, Thompson came after the horse and we lost track of him . . . until we heard that he had been sold in a sheriff's sale, and bought by the Trinchera Ranch east of Alamosa, Colorado. Cliff Fahrion and I went over to see the horse, and realized that the ranch didn't know anything about Cowboy, or how good a horse he was. We got him bought for $175, and took him back to Bayfield . . . this was around 1940. We stood him to mares for $10, and raised it in '42 or '43. That's about when I went into the Army and lost my connections with Cowboy."

Cowboy sired a lot of good horses, and was evidently easy to handle. Says Scott, "We could turn him loose with mares,

This is Little Cowboy, by Cowboy P-12 and out of Show Girl, by Wane of Erie (TB). A sorrel horse foaled in 1946, he was bred, owned, and shown by Fele Fernandez of Alamosa, Colorado. The ID on the back of the picture says: "Champion, Quarter Horse Roping, Denver." **Photo by James Cathey**

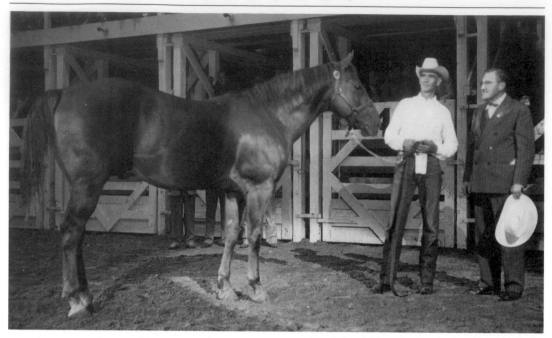

geldings, anything. He'd never bother a mare unless she was in heat. He was the damnedest horse to ride I've ever seen. He was as fast as lightning and could catch a goat or a calf anywhere. And Cowboy himself could be caught anywhere. We didn't need a bucket of grain to get him. He had a grand disposition. Cowboy died at Bayfield when he was 21 or 22," according to Scott.

Clifford Fahrion's son, Howard, who lives in Chama, N.M., remembers that "Dad first became acquainted with Cowboy somewhere between 1930 and 1935. There's always been a controversy about his age and breeding, and I suppose there always will be. Dad bought a Cowboy colt in 1937, and was determined to own Cowboy himself, who had never raced officially but had been matched.

"Dad was always convinced Cowboy was a son of Peter McCue. I can also remember a time when Milo Burlingame (who used to ride Peter McCue) came out from Durango to look at him. Milo, too,

was certain Cowboy had to be by Peter McCue," Howard stated.

"Cowboy was a dark chestnut, almost black. He had a small strip and snip, stood about 15.2 and weighed around 1,200 pounds," Howard continued.

"I'll tell you one thing for sure—he was a broke son-of-a-gun. I handled him when I was 10 or 11 years old. We could do anything on him," Howard summarizes.

Lim Duncan, Durango, Colo., is another who knew Cowboy. "He was an exceptionally nice individual," he recalled. "I don't think he ever raced officially, but he sure sired some runners. As a matter of fact, what Cowboy did was sire some good, solid stock who could do whatever their owners wanted. He came out of New Mexico and, like Shue Fly, a lot of his history was cloudy."

Jim Norton still has the highest respect and admiration for the stallion. "In my opinion, the horse had no faults. I always felt he stood out as the premier sire in those days. He had a wonderful disposition, and he passed it on to his colts."

Don DeMars, another Colorado horseman (from Longmont) whose roots stretch

A 1973 photo of Clifford Fahrion on Cowboy Fahrion, a grandson of Cowboy.

to the Cowboy era, recalled that the dark chestnut stallion was "a good horse. The first Quarter Horse sale at the National Western Stock Show in Denver had some Cowboy colts. They came in rough, but I could still see they were extremely nice individuals and most were out of nothing mares.

"There was a rancher, Fele Fernandez, at Alamosa who was a heck of a roper. He took some Thoroughbred mares to Cowboy and raised Little Cowboy, who was quite a roping pony. I remember he rode him 16 years, and there was never a minute when that horse wasn't well-mannered."

Joe Piz, Golden, Colo., insists "a lot of people never realized just how many

Cowboy horses we had in Colorado. He was an extremely sound horse, and almost all of his colts were the same way.

"Cowboy was on the long-bodied side and not quite as heavy as Quarter Horses were in those days. You could stand there and just look at him, and you knew he was quick. He could gather and go like the devil, and he was about as smooth as glass. Most of his offspring looked like him. I always figured you could tell a Cowboy colt the minute one walked out.

"Cowboy turned out to be a tremendous sire despite not having a lot of high-powered mares, and he left a strong mark in the industry."

14 SHUE FLY

She was noted for her come-from-behind ability.

THIS GRAND mare was, without a doubt, one of the greatest Quarter racing mares of all times. She was the World Champion Quarter Running Horse three times: 1941-42, 1942-43, and 1943-44.

Not only did Shue Fly set track records all over the Southwest, she was noted for her come-from-behind ability to catch the front-runners just before the wire.

This characteristic made people wonder

This photo of Shue Fly clearly shows the patch of roan hairs on her right side.

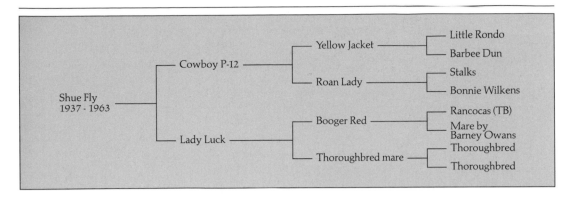

Shue Fly
1937 - 1963
├─ Cowboy P-12
│   ├─ Yellow Jacket
│   │   ├─ Little Rondo
│   │   └─ Barbee Dun
│   └─ Roan Lady
│   ├─ Stalks
│   └─ Bonnie Wilkens
└─ Lady Luck
    ├─ Booger Red
    │   ├─ Rancocas (TB)
    │   └─ Mare by Barney Owans
    └─ Thoroughbred mare
        ├─ Thoroughbred
        └─ Thoroughbred

if she was simply toying with the competition, or if she only ran as fast as she thought was necessary. Whichever, her narrow margins of victory frequently inspired owners of her beaten rivals to try her again, thinking "we can get her next time." But few ever did.

Although there is no doubt about Shue Fly's speed on the track, her breeding will forever remain a controversy. What AQHA recognizes as her official pedigree is shown in the accompanying chart. AQHA's Studbook No. 2, printed in 1943, also lists her breeder as Lloyd Miller, Chamita, N.M., and her owners as the Hepler Brothers, Carlsbad, New Mexico.

However, several old-timers involved with Quarter racing in those early years are unshakable in their belief that Shue Fly was actually sired by a Thoroughbred named Erskine Dale, and that she was out of a Quarter racing mare, Nancy M, by Jack McCue.

At one time, Nancy M was owned by Bob Burris, who later sold the mare to Abe Salazar. As this story of Shue Fly's "unofficial" breeding unfolds, Salazar bred Nancy M to his Thoroughbred stud, Erskine Dale.

Sometime while the mare was in foal, Salazar used her as collateral on a loan. When he couldn't pay off the loan, the man holding the note went to pick up Nancy M. However, Salazar talked him in to waiting a few days, because the mare was so close to foaling. This was in either 1937 or '38.

A couple of days later, the note-holder went to check on the mare, who was pastured in the Animas River valley in southwestern Colorado, in the vicinity of

Halter and Performance Record: Racing Register of Merit; World Champion Quarter Running Mare and World Champion Quarter Running Horse: 1941-42, 1942-43, and 1943-44.

Produce of Dam Record:

Little Fly	1949 mare by Little Joe The Wrangler Racing Register of Merit
Watch Him Fly	1956 gelding by Aldeva (TB)
La Mosquita	1957 mare by Little Request (TB) Racing Register of Merit
Royal Charge	1958 stallion by Depth Charge (TB) Racing Register of Merit

A snapshot of Shue Fly taken at the 1942 New Mexico State Fair in Albuquerque. The handler is unknown. This profile shot indicates why some horsemen felt she looked like she had more Thoroughbred in her than her pedigree indicated. **Photo Courtesy of Jim Norton**

Shue Fly with her colt named Bold Fly, who evidently did not live very long, since the AQHA has no record of him.

Photo Courtesy of Phil Livingston

Elmer Hepler with Shue Fly. Note the patch of roan on the mare's right side, a characteristic said to be typical of Nancy M's foals.

Durango. He found that the mare had foaled, but he could not find the foal.

According to Jim Norton, who lives in Durango, it was speculated that the foal had fallen into the Animas River, since it was springtime and the river was running high from melting snow. Folks believed the foal had drowned.

Yet Norton says he talked to several highway workers on Wolf Creek Pass (east of Durango) not long after that. . . . "and they told me that a Mexican had been stranded in his car, on the pass, during a snowstorm. The workers pulled his car out, but before they left, the Mexican asked for a bottle of milk for his baby."

The workers were startled that this man had no food for his baby, so they rigged a makeshift bottle—and then they were even more startled to find that the baby was actually a relatively newborn foal in the back-seat of the car. Was this Nancy M's missing foal? Many horsemen believe it was.

According to an article in *The Quarter Horse Journal* (June '82), Bob Burris and

Warren Shoemaker were at a track in Trinidad, about 2 years after Nancy M had foaled. They watched a 2-year-old filly run—and as she streaked across the finish line, Burris shouted, "That's Nancy's missing foal!" He said he recognized her because of her uncanny resemblance to Nancy M, and because of a telltale patch of roan on her right side, a characteristic of all of Nancy's foals. The filly, being raced under the name of Spanish Girl, was owned by Abe Salazar.

Burris bought the filly almost immediately, and raced her for several years, very successfully. Somewhere along the line, her name was changed to Shue Fly, but no one seems to know the origin for this name. Burris subsequently sold the mare to the Hepler brothers of Carlsbad, New Mexico. When they applied for her permanent registration number with the AQHA, they listed her breeding as being by Cowboy P-12 and out of Lady Luck.

However, in the aforementioned *QHJ* article, Warren Shoemaker's daughter, Joann Driggers, is quoted: "But in Shoemaker's and Burris' hearts, they knew she was really the lost colt of Nancy M and by Erskine Dale. My father always thought she was the spittin' image of Nancy."

In another *QHJ* article (April '83), author Heidi Bright states: "About 20 years after Shue Fly's birth, according to Driggers, Salazar told only Shoemaker that when Shue Fly was foaled, Salazar took her off Nancy M and put her on Lady Luck, who was then owned by Lloyd Miller. Both Salazar and Miller lived in Espanola, N.M., at that time."

However, the Heplers believed Shue Fly was by Cowboy P-12. So does Howard Fahrion, of Bayfield, Colo., which is not far from Durango. Howard is the son of Clifford Fahrion, who owned Cowboy P-12 in the late '30s. Says Howard: "Lady Luck, Shue Fly's mama, got out and wound up with Cowboy. We didn't plan on the breeding, but it sure worked."

Regardless of her breeding, Shue Fly earned a large niche in Quarter racing history, and is still one of the most respected runners of all time. Old-timers still talk about her legendary ability to

Shue Fly and Little Fly, her 1949 filly by Little Joe The Wrangler, bred by Elmer Hepler.

spot her competitors several lengths, and then roar by them like a freight train. No one ever figured out if she did this deliberately, or if it just took her longer than others to move into high gear.

In one of her greatest races, something happened that no one had planned on: She stumbled coming out of the gates. It was

SHUE FLY
Co-Holder World's Record for 440 Yards

"She stretched her head out about even with her withers and began to sail up that track like a crop-dusting plane."

SHUE FLY, Ch. M. 1937 (AQHA #717) is by Cowboy out of Lady Luck by Booger Red. She was selected as **WORLD'S CHAMPION QUARTER RUNNING HORSE** during the seasons of 1942, 1943 and 1944.

SHUE FLY, who is now retired, is now **IN FOAL** to Bold Venture.

Included in our stables are Black Annie, in foal to Depth Charge, by Bold Venture out of Quickly (Count Fleet's dam), and a number of Quarter Mares, in foal to Just Again by Ariel out of Again by *Teddy, second dam Festive by High Time.

We have some Colts by Old Joe Reed, Tough Company, War Chief and Little Joe the Wrangler (all noted producers of speed).

HELPER BROTHERS
515 North Mesquite Street   **Carlsbad, New Mexico**

This ad appeared in the 1947 American Quarter Racing Association Year Book. Note the misspelling of Hepler; printers had problems with gremlins in those days, too.

in the 1942 World Championship Quarter Mile Race in Arizona. As Shue Fly broke, a hind foot struck a front foot and she went down on her knees. By the time she regained her feet and hit her stride, she was 7 lengths behind. In a quarter-mile race, that's an eternity.

The crowd was aghast at first, then roared, "Come on, Shue Fly!" She shifted into high gear and with her ground-eating stride, caught the others, and won by a nose. The crowd went absolutely wild, and Bob Denhardt later wrote:

"Heart? She had one as big as all outdoors. She stretched her head out about even with her withers and began to sail up that track like a crop-dusting plane . . . making the rest of those rapid-moving ponies look like they were running in reverse."

It was immediately after this race that the Heplers bought her for a reported $3,000, and they continued to race her for several more years. During her career, she defeated such horses as Queenie, Clabber (The "Iron Horse"), Miss Bank, Squaw H, and Nobodies Friend. She got the best of Clabber in a match race, which was particularly unusual because mares seldom won against stallions in match races.

In the 1947 year book of the American Quarter Racing Association, Melville Haskell wrote: "No defeat can ever take away the glory that Shue Fly won during her many years of competition on the quarter tracks. Running only against the top short horses in America, she beat every horse who ever defeated her on a recognized track right up until her last race (which she lost to Miss Princess). She had the great heart and proud courage of a true champion, and won most of her races the hard way—coming from behind in a dazzling burst of speed to catch her competition at the wire."

After Shue Fly lost to Miss Princess in 1947, the Heplers retired her and put her into their breeding program. But as a broodmare, Shue Fly was a disappointment . . . perhaps because, as has been true of some other great racing mares, she gave everything she had on the track, and had nothing left as a broodmare. She proved difficult to get into foal, and of the foals she produced, several died at birth or shortly after.

She only produced two AAA runners: La Mosquita, a filly by Little Request (TB), who won seven races and $8,593; and Royal Charge, by Depth Charge (TB), who won only one race, and earned $1,936.

This grand mare died of old age on the Heplers' ranch in March 1963.

She had the great heart and proud courage of a true champion.

15 HARD TWIST

He was plenty fast, and also one bad hombre.

MENTION THE name of Hard Twist to some of the old-timers, and they will tell you he was a rough, tough race horse who was as hard as nails, and plenty fast. But then they'll pause, and add that he was also one bad hombre. "He was mean as hell," states Jim Norton of Durango, Colo., who has vivid memories of the horse.

Hard Twist was foaled in 1942, and his breeder was either Lou Kirk of Thoreau, N.M., or Cliff Fahrion of Bayfield, Colorado. AQHA Studbook No. 4, published in 1948, lists Kirk as the breeder; yet AQHA's current master ownership record on the horse lists Fahrion as the breeder. A phone call to the AQHA records department reveals that the records on Hard Twist state: "Bred by Lou Kirk; Breeder: Cliff Fahrion."

Jim Goodhue, long-time AQHA registrar who is now retired, offers an explanation for this confusion. He says that on the registration applications used by AQHA in the early days, "Bred by" referred to the owner of the dam at the time of service, and "Breeder" referred to the owner of the stallion. Yet, AQHA has always recognized the owner of the dam as the breeder.

Hard Twist earned a AAA rating and a racing Register of Merit.

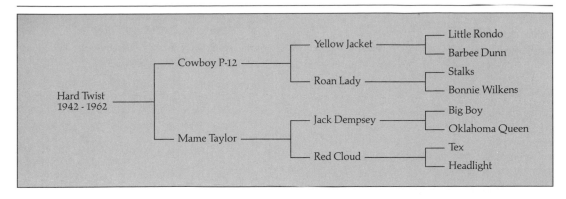

```
                                   ┌── Little Rondo
                     ┌── Yellow Jacket ──┤
                     │             └── Barbee Dunn
          ┌── Cowboy P-12 ──┤
          │          │             ┌── Stalks
          │          └── Roan Lady ──┤
Hard Twist ──┤                      └── Bonnie Wilkens
1942 - 1962  │
          │                        ┌── Big Boy
          │          ┌── Jack Dempsey ──┤
          │          │             └── Oklahoma Queen
          └── Mame Taylor ──┤
                     │             ┌── Tex
                     └── Red Cloud ──┤
                                   └── Headlight
```

Jim adds that the current master record listing Fahrion as the breeder could be an error in the computer entry.

It is known that Lou Kirk did take several mares to be bred to Cowboy P-12, owned by Cliff Fahrion. One of the mares was Hard Twist's dam. She was Mame (sometimes spelled Mamie) Taylor by Jack Dempsey. In his book *Outstanding Modern Quarter Horse Sires*, author Nelson Nye quotes Lou Kirk as saying: "I bought Jack Dempsey from a ranch in Phoenix. He was the fastest Quarter Horse I have ever seen. I ran him mostly in match races, and I ran him so many times I can't remember more than half his races, but he was never defeated. When I retired him to stud, he proved just as great as a sire.

"Mamie Taylor was one of his best. She was so gentle a child could handle her—until she was ready to run a race. Then she would go temperamental and would bite anything or anyone in her way. When she left the score, she *left*. Never in my life have I seen a horse break faster except her sire, Jack Dempsey."

One of the top race horses in the late 1930s, Mamie Taylor had 29 wins, 6 seconds, and 4 thirds in 40 races. And she put a lot of money into the pockets of her owners, Lou and Vivian Kirk.

Hard Twist was probably more "old-time" Quarter Horse than many of his racing contemporaries. His pedigree read that way, and he looked the part. He stood about 14.2 and tipped the scales at 1,100. A good-looking horse, he had a star and a strip, and a sock on the right hind.

Hard Twist got his name from Jim Shirley, who first trained him. In the previously mentioned book, Nelson Nye related, "He (Shirley) said the colt was one of the hardest-twisted, toughest-muscled little horses he had ever seen."

Hard Twist first changed ownership as a

Halter and Performance Record: Racing Register of Merit; 1946 World Champion Quarter Running Stallion; 1951 Co-World Champion Quarter Running Stallion.

Progeny Record:

AQHA Champions: 1	Performance Points Earned: 138.5
Foal Crops: 17	Performance Registers of Merit: 6
Foals Registered: 166	Race Money Earned: $187,926
Halter-Point Earners: 14	Race Registers of Merit: 42
Halter Points Earned: 85	Race Starters: 90
Performance-Point Earners: 9	Superior Race Awards: 6
Leading Race Money Earner: Currency Bee ($22,098)	

2-year-old in 1944 when he was purchased by Wayne Brand, who characterized him as "extremely rank; not mean, but rough and playful."

It was Brand who put Hard Twist's initial running record together. His maiden voyage was a 330-yard race at Corona, California. He wound up racing at tracks in Arizona, Texas, California, Nevada, and New Mexico. When he went to the gates, he went to run.

Before he was retired to stud, he had whipped some of the most prominent names in racing, including Barbra B, Piggin String (TB), Miss Bank, and Tonta Gal. And he had been crowned 1946 Champion Quarter Running Stallion.

Brand gave Hard Twist 18 outs before selling him to Lewis Blackwell of Amarillo, Texas. Blackwell's intention was to retire him to stud. He figured he had a handsome stallion who'd beat some of the best runners on the tracks. Blackwell was confident he'd end up with a crowded book of mares.

Blackwell was wrong. No one remem-

Hard Twist was featured in this ad which appeared in AQHA's Studbook No. 4, published in 1948.

"He was out of a wonderful mare, Mame Taylor."

Hard Twist, 5555

By Cowboy P-12 by Yellow Jacket, and out of Mame Taylor 6990 by Jack Dempsey.

Holder: WORLD'S STALLION RECORD	DEL RIO	440 - 117 - 22.6 f.
Winner: WORLD'S CHAMPIONSHIP STAKES	RIL.	440 - 129 - 22.7 f.
Winner: STALLION STAKES	RIL.	440 - 125 - 22.7 f.
Co-Holder: STALLION RECORD	RIL.	330 - 126 - 17.4 s.

We also own MISS PANAMA 5009, holder of World's Record 330 yards Del Rio - 1948—Time 16.9, and a small but top band of brood mares.

Mr. and Mrs. Lewis M. Blackwell

4201 Bowie   **Phone 8117**   Amarillo, Texas

bers why, but Hard Twist attracted very few mares. Two years later, in 1951, Blackwell, in exasperation, put the stallion back into race training.

People shook their heads and laughed. They thought it was ridiculous that Blackwell thought an 8-year-old could run with the younger, faster, better trained competition of the early '50s. Blackwell let them laugh. So did Walt Harris, who was given Hard Twist to train.

The stallion's first comeback run was over 350 yards in an 11-horse field at Bay Meadows. He finished fifth. Eleven days later, Hard Twist hit the surface again in another 350 with an eight-horse field. He won. Two of the competitors in that group were none other than Leota W and Barred. People stopped laughing.

Several days later, Hard Twist won a 400-yard handicap written for all ages. He won by three-quarters of a length and set a track record.

Two weeks later, Hard Twist finished second by a slim neck in a 400-yarder.

Then, he captured the 400-yard Barbra B Handicap, bettering the previous record by four-tenths of a second. Later, the grand old stallion set another track record when he covered 330 yards in :17.3. He was proclaimed 1951 Co-World Champion Quarter Running Stallion with Bart B.S. and Clabbertown G. It was a heckuva comeback for an aged stallion.

Ed Honnen bought Hard Twist from Blackwell. "He was a champion and I wanted him," said Honnen. "He was out of a wonderful mare, Mame Taylor, and damned if I know where he got his disposition. He was around 10 years old when I bought him.

"At that time, I had a place south of Denver along a ditch bank. We used to ride horses along there for exercise. One day, my trainer was on Hard Twist and I was on one of my riding horses. All of a sudden, Hard Twist reached over and tried to get me. The horse was mean.

"I had 30 to 40 mares of my own, good quality mares. It was a good thing, too, because I couldn't attract many outside mares to Hard Twist. For one thing, people were afraid he'd hurt them. For another,

he had a reputation of putting rather bad-headed babies on the ground.

"Hard Twist was a good, healthy, sound horse," continued Honnen. "He always ate well and took care of himself.

"I lived pretty quietly on the edge of town. That suited Hard Twist just fine. Hard Twist didn't want to see anyone, and no one wanted to see Hard Twist. Usually, he was just fine and caused no trouble if everyone left him alone. Then, again, he had his off days. When that happened, he was absolutely impossible."

Honnen also tells of one quirk Hard Twist had: He absolutely refused to breed a palomino.

Although the horse did have a bad attitude as a mature horse, he evidently was okay in his younger years. "I knew Hard Twist when he was around 2 or so," remembers Joe Piz of Golden, Colorado. "He was full of spunk, but I never thought of him as mean."

After Honnen bought Hard Twist, Piz went to see him. The horse was out in pasture, and Honnen warned Piz to be careful. "I couldn't imagine why Ed was warning me. I told him not to worry. I knew the horse, and thought he would be fine.

"Ed had steps built over the fence into Hard Twist's pasture. I can tell you I sure climbed those steps a lot faster coming out of there than I did going in! I hadn't put a foot inside that enclosure before Hard Twist was after me. I've never run as fast as I did that day.

"*That* Hard Twist, though, was a far different horse from the one I'd known years earlier."

According to the AQHA, Hard Twist's last recorded owner was the Cauble Ranch at Crockett, Texas. The horse died at the age of 20, June 26, 1962, after battling a kidney infection for 2 months. Some of his more famous get include Star Twist, Bar B Twist, Myrtle Twist, Hail Twist, King Twist, and Jenny Twist.

"Hard Twist didn't want to see anyone, and no one wanted to see Hard Twist."

16 HOLLYWOOD GOLD

HOLLYWOOD GOLD is one of the few stallions of renown who spent his entire life on one ranch. He was foaled on the famed 6666 Ranch, specifically that part referred to as the Burnett Estate's Triangle Ranch at Iowa Park, Texas. His breeder is listed as the Tom L. Burnett Cattle Company.

His registration certificate states that he was a dun, but many folks referred to him as a palomino. Much of his breeding is unknown, except for his sire and dam. Gold Rush was a palomino stallion foaled in 1936. Those still around who remember Triangle Lady 17 say that she was a big buckskin mare who had the looks of a Thoroughbred. She was named for the Triangle Ranch, which evidently didn't put much thought into names because there were quite a few mares with the same name—such as Triangle Lady 1, 5, 9, 12, 17, 50, and 67.

This photo of Holly-wood Gold was taken in 1960 when he was 20 years old.

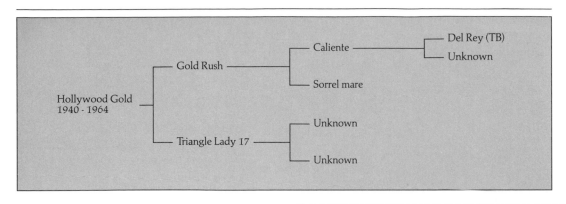

```
                                          ┌─ Del Rey (TB)
                           ┌─ Caliente ───┤
              ┌─ Gold Rush ─┤             └─ Unknown
              │            │
              │            └─ Sorrel mare
Hollywood Gold ┤
1940 - 1964   │
              │                  ┌─ Unknown
              └─ Triangle Lady 17 ┤
                                 └─ Unknown
```

The Triangle Ranch raised a bunch of foals every year, and no one seems to remember anything particularly outstanding about Triangle Lady 17's 1940 foal. He was just another colt . . . until he was tagged with the fancy name of Hollywood Gold.

George Humphreys, the manager of the Sixes, first saw the colt as a yearling when he made a visit to the Triangle. He liked what he saw. Someone else who liked the colt was Anne Burnett Tandy, a granddaughter of S. Burk Burnett and the owner of the vast ranching empire. Always referred to as Miss Anne, she liked the colt as much as George did. When George asked if he could have the colt for his string, Miss Anne replied that she had already selected him to be her personal saddle horse. But, when the colt turned 2, she gave him to George . . . and that marked the beginning of a long relationship between George and the stallion.

From then on, for the most part, Hollywood Gold earned his keep on the Sixes like all the rest of the stallions—he worked cattle and he bred mares.

"We really didn't know what we had in Hollywood Gold," admitted J.J. Gibson, who spent almost as many years with the Four Sixes as George. "I guess we really didn't know how good he was until he was gone, which was 1964.

"I always called him a palomino. He wasn't tall, maybe 14.2, and weighed somewhat over 1,000 pounds. His eyes are what I remember the most about him. They were unbelievably big, pretty, and

Halter and Performance Record: None.

Progeny Record:

AQHA Champions: 1
Foal Crops: 23
Foals Registered: 263
Halter-Point Earners: 9
Halter Points Earned: 35

Performance-Point Earners: 69
Performance Points Earned: 2,787.5
Performance Registers of Merit: 45
Superior Performance Awards: 14

A 1959 photo of two legends: George Humphreys and Hollywood Gold.

Photo by James Cathey

Hollywood Snapper, by Hollywood Gold and out of Miss Tommy 59, was a top cutting horse and earned an NCHA Silver Award. This picture was taken at the 1958 State Fair of Texas where he won the senior cutting and the title of champion cutting horse. Owned at that time by Sonny Braman, Shaker Heights, Ohio, he was ridden by Dale Wilkinson, who later became one of the greats in the reining horse industry. State fair official Donnell C. Clark presents the trophy buckle.

Photo by Squire Haskins

soft. Even mares who still trace to him today have those eyes.

"Hollywood was always good-natured. His colts were the same way, and easy to break. He had tremendous stamina, and good feet and legs. He passed most of his positive qualities on to his offspring.

"Hollywood sired some good sons, but his daughters were the most outstanding. His own daughters, as well as granddaughters, went on to become cutting futurity champions. Matlock Rose won futurities on some of those mares. As a matter of fact, Matlock rode a lot of them.

"Hollywood gave us more than 20

years' worth of offspring. He seemed to work best on Thoroughbred mares. The ranch had quite a few half-Thoroughbreds we'd gotten from the U.S. Remount program. He worked with them, too.

"Most of Hollywood's so-called showing was done at ranch cuttings. We didn't do much other than that. A novice could look at him work and see the cow in him. It was just there. Natural. It wasn't something he was taught because you can't teach it—not the way he did it. He was quick and smart, and could outthink any cow in a hurry.

"He did all of his breeding in pasture. The ranch didn't take in outside mares. We had enough mares to supply our own

At the 1973 Houston Livestock Show and Rodeo, Sonny Paxton of Tallulah, La., won the non-pro cutting on Hollywood Boy, by Hollywood Gold and out of Share A Rose (TB). This palomino gelding was bred by the S.B. Burnett Estate and foaled in 1963.   **Photo by Jim Keeland**

Hollywood Cat, another top cutting horse by Hollywood Gold, won the registered cutting at the Sand Hills Quarter Horse Show in Odessa, Tex., in 1959. He was owned by the Pinehurst Ranch, Orange, Tex., and ridden by John Carter.   **Photo by James Cathey**

needs. We kept some of his babies and sold the rest.

"None of us realized how great that horse was. I don't suppose we even started noticing until we took a good look at how his offspring were working on the ranch. They were just like their daddy. Sure as heck, none of us realized the kind of mark that palomino would leave on the industry, especially in cutting."

And that palomino did, indeed, leave a mark. He sired Hollywood Lin, the 1964 National Cutting Horse Association World Champion Cutting Horse. Both Hollywood Lin and Hollywood Cat were inducted into the NCHA Hall of Fame. And Hollywood Ollie, Hollywood Snapper, and Mr Gold 95 all received NCHA Silver

Awards. Not bad for a horse who came from a long line of unknowns.

He also sired a number of mares who proved to be good producers. One in particular was Miss Hollywood, out of Miss Tommy 86. When Miss Hollywood was bred to Easter King, by King P-234, she produced Hollywood Jac 86. This stallion proved to be a good reining horse and one of the all-time great sires of reining horses.

Hollywood Gold was put down in 1964. He and ol' George have probably hooked up out there somewhere, just cutting a few cows for the fun of it.

BERT

"Just about every roper around wanted a Bert horse."

TALK TO anyone who knew Bert, and the subject will quickly reach two conclusions: 1/ Anyone who swung a rope or wrestled steers in a rodeo arena wanted a Bert offspring; and 2/ anyone who owned a Bert mare was automatically in the horse business.

Foaled in 1934, Bert was bred by Bert Benear of Tulsa. He was by Tommy Clegg and out of Lady Coolidge by Yellow Jacket—also referred to as Beetch's Yellow Jacket. (And Beetch was sometimes spelled as Beech.)

Official AQHA records denote the following progression of ownership for Bert. He was sold by Benear to Bob Weimer of Okmulgee, Okla., in January 1947. Seven months later, he was sold to Winthrop Ingersoll. In May 1950, the brown stallion found a home with G.E. Nicholson of Tulsa. Three years later, in 1953, he found himself with Dell Bryson and, later in 1953, with Earl J. Mayes, who was his last recorded owner. There were also a few stopovers that don't show in the records.

Bert has no AQHA performance record, but he sired four AQHA Champions:

A photograph of Bert, courtesy of Floyd J. "Fifty Thousand" Watts of Tulsa.

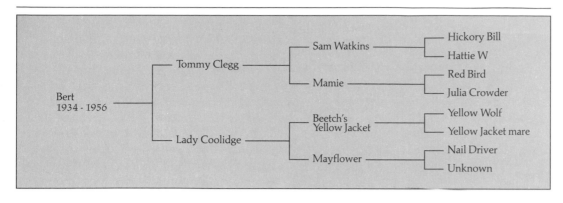

Bert's Lady, Janie Bert Watts, Sutherland's Dwight, and Thomas Bert—who was also AQHA's high-point halter gelding in 1962. Bert also sired Jeanne's Patsy, 1955 AQHA high-point calf roping horse, and 11 horses who earned ROMs in racing.

One of those horsemen who remembers Bert is Nick McNair of Adair, Oklahoma. He says, "I knew Bob Weimer when he stood Bert at Wainwright, Oklahoma. Bert's daughters became some of the most outstanding producers in the country. Just about every roper around wanted a Bert horse, and many of those horses wound up in the hands of some good cowboys. Before long, it was almost a must to cross Bert mares on Oklahoma Star Jr. Bob (Weimer) crossed them on that horse and Little Jodie, and both crosses worked.

"Bert himself was anything but breedy looking, but he sired some extremely pretty daughters. That was surprising to a lot of people since Bert was a cold-blooded, rough-looking stallion."

Many of the Bert/Little Jodie and Oklahoma Star Jr. crosses came about through Ralph Viersen, who owned Star Jr. and Little Jodie. He bought several Bert mares from Bob Weimer and began crossing them on those stallions.

There were several colorful personalities connected with Bert and his offspring. Consider, as one example, Floyd "Fifty Thousand" Watts. During WWII, he traversed Oklahoma selling war bonds with Bob Hope. He introduced Gene Autry at rodeos, and Harry S. Truman at speaking engagements. He's been a rodeo announcer extraordinaire, and been married five times. He also owned Janie Bert Watts—an AQHA Champion daughter of Bert.

He recalls that, "Bert had a bad head, no doubt about that. But put Star Jr. on one of his daughters and the foal turned out great. They all had great back ends, and lots of muscle. There was a tremendous

Halter and Performance Record: None.

Progeny Record:

AQHA Champions: 4	Performance Registers of Merit: 26
Foal Crops: 23	Race Money Earned: $9,749
Foals Registered: 292	Race Registers of Merit: 11
Halter-Point Earners: 33	Race Starters: 17
Halter Points Earned: 438	Superior Halter Awards: 2
Performance-Point Earners: 41	Superior Performance Awards: 3
Performance Points Earned: 545.5	
Leading Race Money Earner: V's Bert ($2,779)	

demand for them, and every cowboy in the country wanted one.

"I can remember one time when I was showing Janie Bert Watts under Leonard Milligan. He walked to me and said, 'Fifty Thousand, take her to the front (of the line). She has a head big enough for two, but a body like a woman.' I took her to the front.

"One year I borrowed $285 to pay my entry fee for a cutting at Fort Worth. I went into the arena on Janie and just dropped the reins on her. We cut a big Brahma who took out running. But that mare dipped her head and bird-dogged him, staying head-to-head with him.

"Bert himself looked about as good as an old plow horse," Watts continues. "He had a deep shoulder and a long underbelly. When Dell Bryson owned him, we had actually bought him together, and sold him 6 months later. We made $1,000 on the deal. Today, $1,000 is about like a bed blanket in a snowstorm, but back then, it was a fortune."

H.V. Roberts was another one connected with the Viersen ranch during the days of Bert and his daughters. "Bert definitely had a bad head," recalled Roberts. "He was low in the back, but had good feet. He was never broke since he had a bad foot that was cut when he was young.

"Today, $1,000 is about like a bed blanket in a snowstorm, but back then, it was a fortune."

"To me, Bonnie Bert was one of the best Bert mares in the country. As a 2-year-old, she finished in a dead heat in the 1949 Oklahoma Futurity, in world record time for 2-year-olds at 200 yards. Viersen bought the horse who dead-heated with her—Grey Question.

"Merry Legs E was another wonderful Bert mare who crossed well on Hysition, a Thoroughbred owned by Viersen. We took her to the New Mexico State Fair in the fall of 1951. She ran AA time for us, and we'd

just weaned her colt off her in June of that year. Some of Merry Legs E's daughters went on to make great broodmares."

Roberts continues: "I think one of the greatest mares Bert ever sired was Beauty W, who was out of a mare by Oklahoma Star, who was referred to as the Bald-Faced Mare. Bill and Jeannie Moore of Broken Arrow, Okla., owned her. They bred Beauty W to Little Jodie and got Beauty Jo. Beauty Jo won so many show trophies that they filled one huge space in the Moores' home.

"No one can doubt that Bert was a strong breeder. His daughters crossed well with just about anything, but the best were the Star Jr. and Little Jodie crosses. I can tell you his offspring were in great demand. Cowboys knew they were a-horseback if they could get a Bert under them. Even today, you can see the Bert blood showing up four and five generations back in pedigrees.

"He was consistent as a breeder, and you could almost always recognize his daughters. He could have been one of the greatest Quarter Horse sires in the industry if he had just put a good head on his offspring. Even so, he was ahead of his time as a sire."

In addition to Bert's sons and daughters making names for themselves, there was a granddaughter who carved a large niche for herself in rodeo history. This was Baby Doll, registered as Baby Doll Combs. Foaled in 1947, she was by Oklahoma Star Jr. and out of a Bert daughter, Miss Boctick.

Baby Doll was owned by Willard Combs, one of the nation's top steer wrestlers in the 1950s. He not only competed on Baby Doll, but also let other cowboys bulldog steers on this great mare (for a percentage of their winnings). Anyone who rode her was almost a sure bet to finish in the money. In 1955, for example, cowboys 'dogging off Baby Doll won $56,000 . . . and in 1957, $75,500. Also in '57, Willard won the R.C.A. world championship in steer wrestling riding Baby Doll. When she died in 1960, her loss was felt throughout rodeo.

Baby Doll was a testimonial for an old saying about Bert mares that was popular in the late 1930s and on through the '50s: "If you had a Bert mare, you knew you were in the horse business."

AQHA records show that Bert died in May 1956, at the age of 22.

TOP DECK (TB) 18

TOP DECK was another Thoroughbred who had a tremendous impact on the Quarter Horse industry. There was absolutely no question that he could sire speed, and his sons and daughters, and their descendants, dominated on the track and in

He was a royally bred horse who could sire speed.

Top Deck.

Photo by James Cathey

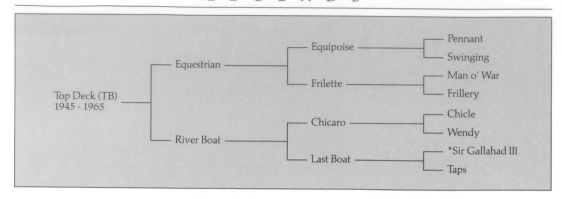

Top Deck (TB)
1945 - 1965
- Equestrian
  - Equipoise
    - Pennant
    - Swinging
  - Frilette
    - Man o' War
    - Frillery
- River Boat
  - Chicaro
    - Chicle
    - Wendy
  - Last Boat
    - *Sir Gallahad III
    - Taps

Halter and Performance Record: None.

Progeny Record:

AQHA Champions: 4
Foal Crops: 19
Foals Registered: 440
Halter-Point Earners: 17
Halter Points Earned: 152
Performance-Point Earners: 21
Performance Points Earned: 407.5
Leading Race Money Earner: Top Ladybug ($195,943)

Performance Registers of Merit: 12
Race Money Earned: $1,680,769
Race Registers of Merit: 219
Race Starters: 341
Superior Race Awards: 21
Supreme Champions: 2
World Champions (Racing): 5

arena speed events. But, if it hadn't been for J.B. Ferguson of Wharton, Tex., Top Deck might have lived his life in relative obscurity.

Ferguson had a keen eye for a horse. In fact, his grandson, Kip Attaway, says, "Anyone who knew my grandfather will tell you he had an unbelievable knack for recognizing quality horseflesh. It was like something magic. He could look, and he would know. It was like an extra sense for him. He took a gamble when he paid $25,000 for Top Deck. It was a risk, but I don't think it was as much of a risk for him as it would have been for someone else. Why? Because, as I said, he could see more than anyone else.

"We had a lot of great horses. There was Diamond Mae and many more, but they all seemed to stand in the shadows of Top Deck and his son, Go Man Go."

Had it not been for Ferguson's keen eye, and also his willingness to gamble, it's likely Top Deck would have fallen

through the industry cracks. Here's how it all happened.

Top Deck was royally bred. He was by Equestrian, who was by the gallant Equipoise.

Owned by C.V. Whitney, Equipoise retired sound after going to the post 51 times. His record reflected 29 firsts, 10 seconds, and 4 thirds. His career at stud ended after only four seasons due to an untimely death caused by an intestinal infection. The offspring he left behind, however, placed him among the top horses on the 1942 Thoroughbred sire list.

Robert Kleberg Jr., of King Ranch fame, had watched Equipoise, and was determined to have one of his sons. He made good his intent when he purchased Equestrian, who was out of Frilette by Man o' War. Unfortunately, Kleberg experienced even worse luck than Whitney when Equestrian died after breeding only a handful of mares.

One of the mares was River Boat. She was by Chicaro, who was also owned by the King Ranch, and out of Last Boat by *Sir Gallahad III. The product of the mating between Equestrian and River Boat was Top Deck, foaled in 1945. His pedigree was saturated with the Commando/Ben Brush cross which, even today, is held in high esteem.

Would the chain of bad luck be broken with Top Deck? No . . . at least not for a while. No one is absolutely certain what happened because there were no eyewitnesses, but it's said that Top Deck was kicked in the knee when very young. He would never make it to a starting gate, and the King Ranch either sold him or gave him to a good friend of Kleberg's, Ernest Lane, of Odem, Texas. One story says that the ranch sold him; another says the horse was a gift to Lane. No one today can verify which account is true.

Top Deck's papers were officially transferred to Lane on June 1, 1948, even though Lane had the horse before that. The signature representing the King Ranch in the transfer was that of their long-time veterinarian, Dr. J.K. Northway.

Evidently Dr. Northway liked the horse, because he contacted J.B. Ferguson to tell him about Top Deck. Ferguson, an oilman, must have liked what he heard, because he subsequently bought the horse, from Lane, for a reported $25,000, a lot of money for an unsound and unproven stallion. But, Ferguson was known for his sixth sense about horses. After buying the horse, Ferguson moved him to his J Bar F Ranch at Wharton, southwest of Houston.

Because Wharton was well off the beaten path for breeders, Ferguson later moved Top Deck to A.B. Green's place at Purcell, Oklahoma. Initially, he did not receive many mares. Says Joan Attaway, Ferguson's daughter and Kip's mother, "At first, many breeders shunned Top Deck. I guess my father took one risk after another. He was surprised when he had trouble getting mares to Top Deck in Wharton. He decided to change the situation, which is why he moved the horse to Oklahoma. About a year later, he sold half-interest in him to A.B. Green.

"I can remember when he came home with a gray mare from Louisiana," Joan continued. "Her name was Lightfoot Sis. He paid $300 for her, bred her to Top Deck, and she produced Go Man Go. He bought another mare on that same trip. He paid $300 for her. She was originally named Moonlight, but Daddy changed it to Moonlight Night. When bred to Top Deck, she produced Moon Deck, who sired the great Jet Deck.

"I can also remember when Go Man Go was on the to-be-gelded list three times. Each time they started to do it, Daddy changed his mind—thank goodness," Joan laughs.

"Daddy was a wildcatter. He was accustomed to taking risks. His father was a sharecropper, and knew what it was to be poor. They rode horses just about everywhere, and I suppose that's where Daddy first picked up that special feel of his. He always told us the important thing was to get a good bloodline, and then find the right nick."

Top Deck nicked well with many mares, and he certainly was prepotent in passing on his speed. But, he also passed on his rank disposition. Even today, trainers such as Bubba Cascio insist that the Top Deck disposition is still evident several generations later. Cascio, who has trained hundreds of horses, remembers when he first got Windy Ryon (by Go Man Go by Top Deck). "He was no different than any of the other Top Deck horses," he laughed. "Rank as heck until you finally get them broke. Even today, they're a handful to handle."

Go Man Go is remembered as one of the rankest and most difficult to handle. Joan Attaway adds, "All the Top Deck sons, from Go Man Go on, took after Top Deck, and he never sired anything that was easy to control. I always called Moon Deck an outlaw. He'd flip in the gate and do just about anything else."

In addition to the horses already mentioned, Top Deck's roster of stars included Decketta, Miss Top Flame, Rapid Deck, Barbara 3, Top Lady Bug, Rebel Cause, Flight Deck, Astro Deck (who became an AQHA Supreme Champion), and dozens of others who earned their ROM in racing. His sons became outstanding sires, and his daughters became outstanding producers.

It was 1965 when Top Deck became ill. Word was sent to Ferguson, who chartered a plane and flew to Purcell. A team of five veterinarians were at A.B. Green's farm, but they couldn't save the rank old stallion. He was buried at Green Pastures.

But Top Deck still lives through his offspring. He might be three or four or five generations back in a pedigree, but he's there.

Trainers insist that the Top Deck disposition is still evident several generations later.

19 GO MAN GO

He was one of the mightiest speedsters to ever roar down a track.

GO MAN GO, a distinctive strawberry roan Quarter Horse stallion, was one of the mightiest speedsters to ever roar down a track. And he was just as mighty when he was retired to stud. Names of his sons and daughters are forever etched in the memory of Quarter racing fans. Horses such as Duplicate Copy, Go Derussa Go, Go Josie Go, Goetta, Hustling Man, Mr. Meyers, Dynago Miss, and Go Coon Go are but a few who raced to fame and glory.

AQHA records show that Go Man Go's sons and daughters earned over $7 million, and that was back in the days when purses were not as lucrative as they later became.

Go Man Go was foaled in 1953. He was by Top Deck and out of Lightfoot Sis, a mare that J.B. "Johnny" Ferguson had picked up in Louisiana for the humble

Go Man Go, one of the greatest.

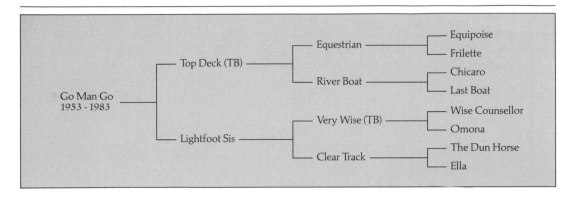

price of $300. She was by Very Wise (TB), and was in the AQHA Appendix registry.

Ferguson, a race horse man, was a friend of Ernest Lane, who was standing the royally bred Top Deck (TB) in the late 1940s. He first sent a mare named Skippy F to the court of Top Deck, and in 1948 she produced Star Deck F, who went on to win the first West Texas Futurity at Del Rio in 1950. Skippy F eventually produced seven AAA runners by Top Deck. But in the meantime, Ferguson also sent Lightfoot Sis to him. Her second breeding to Top Deck resulted in Go Man Go.

The roan colt was foaled on Ferguson's ranch at Wharton, Tex., and began earning a reputation as a rogue long before he got to the racetrack. Robert Strauss was one of the first men to realize that Go Man Go would prove to be a handful. A lifelong horseman, he had been a jockey for years, and was breaking colts for Ferguson when it was time to start the roan under saddle. In an article about Go Man Go in *Western Horseman* (July 1990), Strauss was quoted as follows:

"I put a new halter and lead rope on him to take him to the barn. He broke both of them and took off before we got there. He ran like a bullet. He later bucked off a stock saddle while he was tied to the fence. He pawed Elridge in the paddock. (Elridge Strauss was Robert's brother and Ferguson's trainer.) It took me forever to get up enough nerve to get on that horse the first time, and I'd been riding all my life. I guarantee you he had buck on his mind every morning.

"We spent 60 days snubbing him up and then leading him and riding him in the lot. Well, one morning Elridge and I looked at one another. We were both thinking the same thing—we'd never get him to the racetrack at this rate! I finally got on him and Elridge unsnubbed him,

Halter and Performance Record: 1955, 1956, 1957 World Champion Quarter Running Horse; 1955, 1956, 1957 Champion Quarter Running Stallion; 1955 Champion Quarter Running 2-Year-Old Colt; 1956 Champion Quarter Running 3-Year-Old Colt.

Progeny Record:

AQHA Champions: 7	Race Money Earned: $7,631,518
Foal Crops: 21	Race Registers of Merit: 552
Foals Registered: 942	Race Starters: 775
Halter-Point Earners: 16	Superior Halter Awards: 2
Halter Points Earned: 268	Superior Performance Awards: 4
Performance-Point Earners: 25	Superior Race Awards: 72
Performance Points Earned: 490.5	World Champions (Racing): 7
Performance Registers of Merit: 13	
Leading Race Money Earner: Vim And Vigor ($309,831)	

and that son-of-a-gun took off. I expected him to be fast, but not that fast!"

Go Man Go stayed fast, and he stayed ornery, and his first official race would never be forgotten by those who were there. It took place in May 1955 at Los Alamitos in southern California. Ferguson was still his owner, Elridge was the trainer, and William Strauss was the jockey. Said Robert, the colt's most frequent rider, "I would have been on him, but Elridge and I had a fight before we got to Los Al, and he wouldn't let me ride, so my brother rode him in his first race."

There were eight horses in the race, with Go Man Go the betting favorite by virtue of some earlier works. All horses were in the gate and ready, but before the starter could turn the field loose, Go Man Go reared, threw his jockey, broke through the gate, and flew down the track. He continued flying until he was finally apprehended. The crowd roared as

If ever a horse loved the sheer joy of running, it was Go Man Go. Robert Strauss, the rider in this photo, had the unenviable job of breaking the fractious roan, but then piloted him to many of his wins.

Photo by Jack Stribling

"He ran as fast by himself as he did in competition."

the roan was put back into the gate.

When the gates opened officially, Go Man Go sprinted to the front and won . . . making history by running two races within one 30-minute period.

Go Man Go wrapped up his first season by being named 1955 World Champion Quarter Running Horse, Champion Quarter Running Stallion, and Champion Quarter Running 2-Year-Old. He was the first 2-year-old named world champion and, by that time, his owner was listed as A.B. Green.

Green's wife, Kathlyn, said Ferguson and her husband were long-time friends. "Johnny (Ferguson) approached A.B. about buying Go Man Go. A.B. certainly liked him, but he really didn't know if he wanted to buy him.

"A.B. went to Los Alamitos to watch Go Man Go run. He liked what he saw, and he finally bought him for $40,000, which was a tremendous sum."

When A.B. Green became Go Man Go's owner, training duties for the incredible roan passed from Elridge Strauss to Wade Johnson. In 1956, at Ruidoso, N.M., Johnson hooked the stallion back up with Robert Strauss.

"Boom!" laughed Robert. "That horse ran and was unbeaten during the meet. He was a king!" In 1956 he was declared

World Champion Quarter Running Horse and Champion Stallion again, and also Champion 3-Year-Old Colt.

The colt was taken back to Los Alamitos, and then to Bay Meadows, "but the track couldn't fill a race if people knew he was entered," Robert continued. "No one wanted to run against him. Finally, we worked him alone for the public. And you know what? He ran as fast by himself as he did in competition. That's the way he was. There was no stopping him."

The year 1957 was Go Man Go's 4-year-old season, and he was named world champion for the third time as well as champion stallion. He was still running strong as a 6-year-old in 1959.

"What can anyone say about a horse like Go Man Go," mused Robert more than 30 years after the horse's retirement from the track. "He was ornery from the first day I met him, but he was the greatest horse I ever rode. As a matter of fact, he was one of the greatest horses that ever lived. No one can doubt that. He became a legend while he was on the track, and he added to it as a sire. Somehow, *great* doesn't sound like an important enough word for him."

Go Man Go was retired to Green's Green Pastures, near Purcell, Okla., where he continued to set records. In addition to the horses already mentioned, he also sired such greats as Windy Ryon, Whataway To Go, Laderago, Sold Short, Some Kinda

122

A 1956 photo of Go Man Go with A.B. Green (left) and Johnny Ferguson, when Green bought the roan from Ferguson for $40,000.

Man, Moore Go, and Off Limits. He also sired the dams of Kaweah Bar, Mr. Kid Charge, Rocket Wrangler, Ettago Chickie, and Six Te. The roan stallion was officially listed as the leading sire of money earners in 1971, 1972, 1976, and 1977.

Go Man Go's history as a breeding horse wasn't without controversy. Initially, the AQHA refused to issue him a registration number. In his book, *They Rode Good Horses*, which chronicles the history of the AQHA, author Don Hedgpeth wrote:

"Green sought to have the horse advanced in the AQHA registry from Appendix to Tentative, knowing this would enhance his appeal as a horse to whom to breed, once he left the track. But the mare Lightfoot Sis had died without advancing out of the Appendix, and it was generally agreed that, while Go Man Go might qualify on the Register of Merit, he would never pass on conformation inspection. He looked like what he was, 'mostly Thoroughbred.'

"The dilemma facing the association's

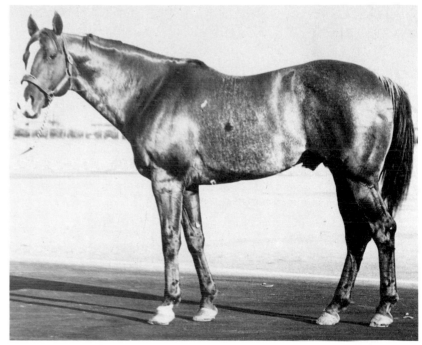

Another photo of the strawberry roan, depicting him in racing shape.
Photo by Darol Dickinson, Courtesy of Maggie Clark

123

Windy Ryon, a AAA son of Go Man Go, out of Silent Light, by Dividend, was foaled in 1973. He earned a Superior title in racing, and went on to sire 829 foals, of which 252 earned an ROM in racing.

Goetta, AAAT, one of Go Man Go's best daughters, was foaled in 1961, out of Etta Leo, a AA daughter of Leo. Goetta won many racing titles, as well as the 1963 All-American Futurity.

executive committee was whether to advance him to a numbered registration and reap the benefits of all the positive relations he had generated, or stand firm and repudiate him on the grounds of his Thoroughbred conformation and origins."

In 1956, the executive committee took no action. In 1957, the committee again declined to act, deciding to wait and see what Go Man Go's first crop of foals looked like. Not until 1958 did the committee finally issue a number—No. 82,000—to the roan legend.

"So much has been said about Go Man Go," mused Kathlyn Green. "Some of it is true and some of it isn't. He was always thought of as a rogue. Maybe he was, but I know how he was here at the farm. He'd lean his head over the stall door and stand there all day if someone would just stand with him and pull on his lip, which he liked. One of the quirks I remember the most about him was he absolutely hated getting his feet dirty.

"A.B. stood Go Man Go in 1958 and 1959. We had a pretty good crop from that second year but, as luck would have it, a virus tore through our barn. We lost just about everything. I don't think I'd ever seen A.B. as discouraged as he was then. He just couldn't bear to see another colt die.

"Les Gosselin of Oklahoma City always had an eye for Go Man Go. Gosselin wanted to buy him and A.B., down about as far as he could go over losing all those babies, agreed to sell. I can tell you he regretted making the deal as soon as the words were out of his mouth, but he never tried to renege. He went ahead, and that's how Les came to own the horse."

Less than one year later, Bill and Harriett Peckham, along with Frank Vessels Sr. bought the strawberry roan. After Vessels died, his son, Frank Jr., sold the Vessels' interest to Melvin Hatley. The horse's ownership after that is tangled, but Harriett Peckham finally became the sole owner, bringing the roan stallion to her Buena Suerte Ranch at Roswell, N.M., in 1972. He died October 14, 1983, at Peckham's ranch. He was 30 years old.

DEPTH CHARGE 20
(TB)

DEPTH CHARGE was a Thoroughbred who ran like a Quarter Horse, and sired a number of outstanding Quarter Horse runners. He was also owned by many people during his lifetime. Perhaps the best place to begin his story is with a look at Depth Charge's sire, Bold Venture.

It was March 4, 1933, when Bold Venture was foaled at Morton L. Schwartz's Elsmeade Stud in Kentucky. Later, Schwartz turned over the training of Bold Venture to Max Hirsch, Thoroughbred trainer for the King Ranch. In 1935,

Schwartz became disenchanted and discouraged with the world of racing, and decided to disperse his stock. Bold Venture was led into the sales ring, but commanded only modest bidding. Schwartz decided to keep the colt.

Bold Venture was pointed toward the starting gate for his maiden race on June 1, 1935. He was as green as grass and lost by 4 lengths. He entered his next race 4 weeks later and won by a head. The colt was obviously a quick learner with a great deal of speed. But he went through his

Depth Charge was a Thoroughbred who ran like a Quarter Horse.

Elmer Hepler once said that Depth Charge was "the smoothest, most well-muscled, and best-looking son-of-a-gun you ever looked at."

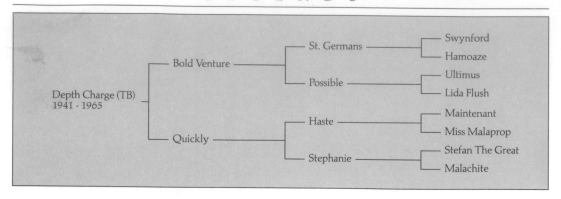

Halter and Performance Record: None.

Progeny Record:

AQHA Champions: 3	Performance Points Earned: 12
Foal Crops: 20	Performance Registers of Merit: 1
Foals Registered: 220	Race Money Earned: $583,467
Halter-Point Earners: 11	Race Registers of Merit: 80
Halter Points Earned: 113	Race Starters: 115
Performance-Point Earners: 1	World Champions (Racing): 4
Leading Race Money Earner: Tiny Charger ($74,482)	

first year on the track with more downs than ups.

The stallion returned to competition as a 3-year-old, and on May 2, 1936, ran in the Kentucky Derby. He was a betting long shot and, in the first few furlongs, he seemed doomed to fail. He and his 18-year-old apprentice jockey, Ira Hanford, got away next to last in the field of 14. But by the time they reached the half-mile pole, the kid and the long shot were ahead by a length. They were never headed from that point to the finish.

Bold Venture's next engagement was the Preakness, which he won with an awesome burst of speed and power in the last furlong.

The horse then went into training for the Belmont. He was progressing well until he bowed a tendon less than 2 weeks before the final Triple Crown competition. He was retired to the breeding barn with $68,300 in earnings.

After Bold Venture won the Derby, he was purchased by the King Ranch, and it was at the ranch's Kentucky division that he stood at stud.

Depth Charge was foaled in March 1941 at Mrs. John D. Hertz's Leona Farm in Carey, Illinois. He was out of a black mare named Quickly. As soon as Depth Charge was weaned, the King Ranch purchased him and hauled him to their Texas ranch at Kingsville. The ranch had also considered buying Quickly, but the sale fell through when the mare was led out of her stall wearing a cribbing halter.

It was trainer Max Hirsch who took over Depth Charge as a 2-year-old. Hirsch, who also trained Bold Venture, expected Depth Charge to be comparable to his sire. But he discovered that Depth Charge was a Thoroughbred who ran like a Quarter Horse. He was incapable of going the more classic and accepted Thoroughbred distances. World War II was in full swing by the time Depth Charge began competing. It was during this period that racetracks in the United States temporarily ended racing. As a result, many well-respected runners, including Depth Charge, were transported to Mexico City, where they continued their racing careers.

Depth Charge was retired after earning nearly $75,000 (most of it in Mexico), and entrusted to John Dial of Goliad, Tex., the same man who earlier had sold King Ranch the famed Chicaro (TB). The first year the brown stallion stood at stud was 1947. It also signified the continuation of what was becoming the stallion's geographical odyssey.

Two of the first horsemen to show their faith in Depth Charge were Elmer and Charlie Hepler of Arizona. They brought Black Annie to him during his first season, and she produced, in 1948, Johnny Dial, who became the 1952 World Champion Quarter Running Horse. The Heplers were two of the most highly regarded individuals in the early Quarter racing industry. They owned, among others, the immortal Shue Fly, and the brothers wanted to breed Shue Fly to Depth Charge. They'd already tried to breed her to Bold Venture, but the mare, who had some age on her, did not settle. They decided to try Depth Charge, thinking he'd be a more aggressive breeder than his sire. They were right.

Shue Fly conceived and produced a handsome sorrel colt. Unfortunately, he died of a twisted intestine.

Elmer Hepler, when talking about Depth Charge, was once quoted as saying, "He was the smoothest, most well-muscled, and best-looking son-of-a-gun you ever looked at."

Depth Charge remained at Goliad, Tex., through the 1950 breeding season. Then he was moved to the King Ranch's Kentucky division. That, unfortunately, was a tactical error in terms of Depth Charge as a sire of Quarter Horses. He stood in Kentucky through 1957, and wound up with only one Quarter Horse foal to represent him from that period. He did no better with the Thoroughbreds, since his pedigree simply was not considered fashionable by Kentuckians.

Meanwhile, several Depth Charge offspring were racing in Texas and Louisiana. They became the scourge of the straightaways and the talk of every local cafe. They were, in a word, fast. The earlier names included Brigand, a Thoroughbred who earned nearly $46,000 and the title of World Champion Quarter Running Gelding in 1952, '53, and '54. There was Dividend, who eventually wound up at the Phillips Ranch in Texas and became a sire in his own right. He was out of Diamond Chick by Chicaro (TB). His earnings at retirement came to nearly $31,000. There were Johnny Dial (out of Black Annie by Rodney by Old D.J.); Super Charge (out of O'Quinn Midget by King), who was 1953 Quarter Running Champion 2-Year-Old; and Chudej's Black Gold (out of Mabel Crawford by Chicaro Bill). They were all good. They were all fast. But there were virtually no more Depth Charge offspring coming along.

At the age of 16, Depth Charge was shipped to California, to start over as a Quarter Horse sire. He was purchased by film star Audie Murphy. When the stallion was led from the plane, with him was a stubbornly hateful goat by the name of Ellsworth. The two were inseparable.

Depth Charge with Ellsworth the goat, his constant companion for years.

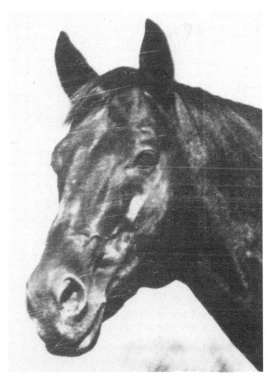

A head shot of Depth Charge.

The horse was to stand at a ranch owned by Gordon Shultz, a friend of Elmer Hepler. Shultz had been able to buy a percentage of the horse—in partnership with Murphy. Hepler lost no time taking Shue Fly to Shultz. He left the mare there with the understanding she would be bred to Depth Charge for as long as she lived. She settled to the stallion and produced Royal Charge (AAA). She settled to him again and produced twins. Both died. They also marked the last foals produced by the great mare.

127

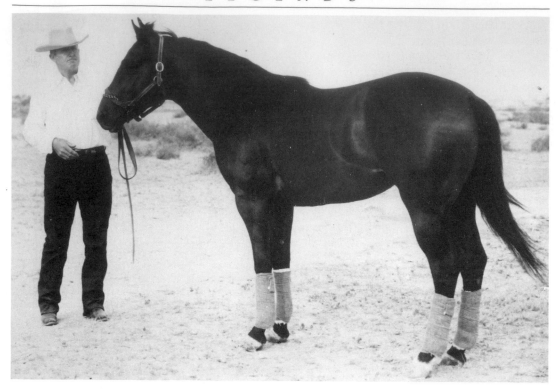

Johnny Dial was one of Depth Charge's best sons. The horse, held by Elmer Hepler, was a 2-year-old in training when this photo was taken.

Hugh Huntley bought Depth Charge in 1960. Sid Huntley, Hugh's son, then moved the stallion to Madera, Calif., on February 16, 1961. Depth Charge was 20 years old and Ellsworth the goat was still by his side.

That all happened years ago, but Sid Huntley remembers both the horse and the goat well. "I was the one who actually stood Depth Charge," he recalled. "As things turned out, I also had to handle Ellsworth.

"Depth Charge was definitely a good-looking individual. He had good bone, good disposition, and the best feet of any horse I'd ever seen. They were just like flint. I always said any colt within three generations of him had those same hard, black feet.

"Ellsworth was a huge African goat with no horns—thank goodness. He was always with the stallion. He'd butt Depth Charge in the belly, and the horse would reach around and grab him. If the situation got serious, Depth Charge would pick up Ellsworth so his feet were barely touching the ground. The goat would scream like crazy until Depth Charge put him down."

What attracted Hugh Huntley to Depth Charge in the first place? "We knew about Brigand, Johnny Dial, and Chudej's Black Gold. After we saw Chudej's Black Gold run, we were definitely impressed. Chudej's

Black Gold was stout with a long hip. He was good-looking. Dad also knew Elmer Hepler, and it was common knowledge how he felt about Depth Charge.

"I told Dad that Chudej's Black Gold would definitely be the stud to get if we could buy him. Well, Dad had turned around and managed to get Depth Charge himself. He certainly one-upped me there.

"Depth Charge was far ahead of his time. He was a great horse then, and he'd be a great horse today. Very few people realized, back then, just how influential he'd be in terms of pedigree. One of the basic problems: We had only a handful of people who knew how to train Depth Charge offspring. They were hot-blooded and somewhat flighty, but I never had a Depth Charge foal who tried to kick or strike. They would run over you, though, if you stood in their way. As far as they were concerned, that was the easiest way to go from point A to point B."

One of Depth Charge's best sons was Tiny Charger, foaled in 1960 out of the mare Clabber Tiny. He carved a AAAT rating on the track and sired a number of outstanding horses who earned ROMs in racing.

When Depth Charge began getting on in years, he developed breeding problems. He no longer seemed able to settle mares. The Huntleys were reluctant to sell the stallion, but as Sid said, "Dad didn't want

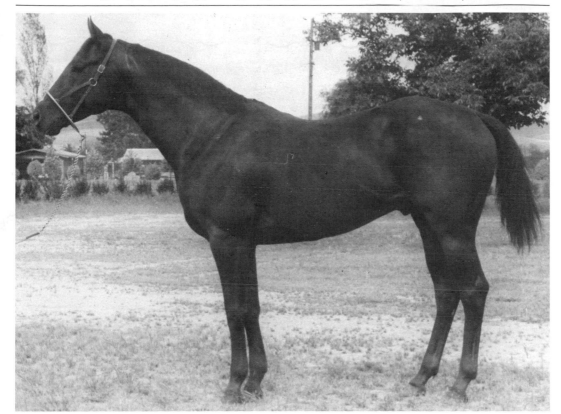

Dividend, a 1951 son of Depth Charge rated AAAT on the track. He became a leading sire of Quarter running horses. The horse was owned by John Taylor, Chino, Calif., when this picture was taken.

Photo by John Williamson, Courtesy of Phil Livingston

to sell him, but he knew, if he kept him, he'd spend all this time trying to breed him. We decided it was better to let him go."

So, the stallion was 22 years old and moving again. This time, his owners were listed as E.K. "Tiny" Johnston of Amarillo, Tex., and Bob Moore Jr., of Grand Prairie, Texas. The stallion stood in Tulsa, Okla., under the care of Dr. R.K. King.

King made some drastic changes in Depth Charge's life. For one thing, he removed the aging but still rambunctious Ellsworth, giving him to some nearby people. He replaced Ellsworth by putting a pregnant mare in Depth Charge's stall.

"At first," said King, "he wanted to savage the mares. We got him over that. After the mare was heavy in foal, I'd replace her with another one. The stallion was really easy to keep. He settled down and took to having a mare with him. Strangely enough, the only ones we ever got in foal to him were first-foal mares."

King exercised extreme care and patience while Depth Charge was with him. The result was seven foals registered by the stallion in 1965.

"Depth Charge was a gallant, big horse with big bone. He stood 16 hands and was extremely good-looking," remembers King.

Though he was probably worn out,

Depth Charge once again was moved. This time, it was 1964 and he was taken to E.K. Johnston's ranch at Shamrock, Texas. Dr. King talked to the people who had the cantankerous Ellsworth. They were only too happy to relinquish the goat, who had an unsavory penchant for digging up everyone's roses. The big, hornless African rejoined Depth Charge. The two old friends made the trek to Shamrock together.

Depth Charge died at Shamrock in 1965. When that happened, the life seemed to flow from Ellsworth as well. The goat lost his zest for living, and died a few months later.

The brown stallion overcame virtually all obstacles in terms of becoming a noteworthy sire. His influence is still felt in countless racing pedigrees, and it even spilled into show and performance through offspring such as Three Deep, Depth Bars, David Cox, Dynamite Charge, Mr. Charge, Bob Charge, Short Charge, Todd's Charge, and Dallas County. He traveled from one coast to the other. Each step he took seemed to leave lasting imprints in the Quarter Horse industry. In 1991, his contributions were recognized when he was inducted into the American Quarter Horse Hall of Fame.

21

PLAUDIT

"All his colts had speed. We could breed him to a Percheron and get something that was fast."

Plaudit was 21 years old when this picture was taken.

Photo by Hellbusch

PLAUDIT WAS a palomino horse , foaled in 1930 in Colorado, whose name appears frequently in the pedigrees of many renowned Quarter Horses . . . horses such as Skipper's Lad, Scooter W, Question Mark, and Gold Mount.

As shown in his pedigree, Plaudit had a lot of Thoroughbred on the top side. His paternal grandsire, Plaudit, achieved lasting fame by winning the Kentucky Derby in 1898. Unfortunately, his success as a sire did not match his success on the

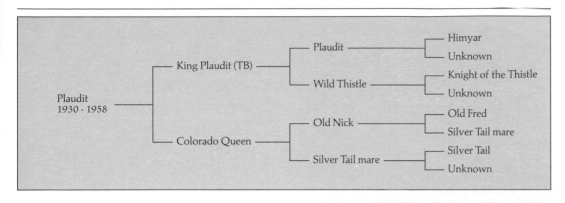

Plaudit
1930 - 1958

King Plaudit (TB)

Plaudit
— Himyar
— Unknown

Wild Thistle
— Knight of the Thistle
— Unknown

Colorado Queen

Old Nick
— Old Fred
— Silver Tail mare

Silver Tail mare
— Silver Tail
— Unknown

track. Nonetheless, he sired some decent colts, such as King Plaudit.

This seal brown colt won five races out of thirteen starts, the last being in New York in 1919. After that, he was shipped to the Arthur Wilbur ranch in western Colorado where he was used as an Army Remount stallion.

One of the mares brought to his court was Colorado Queen, owned by Tom Mills of Meeker, Colorado. She had been bred by Coke Roberds of Hayden, Colo., who achieved recognition through his stallions, Old Fred and Peter McCue. Horsemen who still remember this dun mare say there wasn't anything on four legs that could catch her on the bush tracks.

Her pedigree was interesting, to say the least. She was by Old Nick, who was out of a Silver Tail mare. This is possibly the same mare listed as Colorado Queen's dam. If it is, Old Nick was bred back to his dam, and the resulting foal was Colorado Queen.

The result of the breeding of Colorado Queen to King Plaudit was a palomino colt foaled July 8, 1930. Mills named the good-looking colt after his paternal grand-sire, Plaudit.

The colt began changing hands when he was just 3 months old. His first buyer was Coke Roberds, who had always liked Colorado Queen, and who especially liked the palomino colt. He paid $250 for him, a fancy price in those days for such a young colt. Roberds then sold the colt as a yearling to Jack Hauskins. Hauskins, in turn, sold him a few months later to Warren Shoemaker of Watrous, N.M.,

Halter and Performance Record: None.

Progeny Record:

Foal Crops: 28	Performance-Point Earners: 6
Foals Registered: 187	Performance Points Earned: 7
Halter-Point Earners: 2	World Champions (Racing): 1
Halter Points Earned: 4	

who was partial to yellow horses.

But when Plaudit was 3, Shoemaker sold him to Waite Phillips, who owned the 130,000-acre Philmont Ranch out of Cimmaron, New Mexico. Phillips really liked the horse, and Shoemaker, as he said later, really needed the money. He also had two stallions—Nick and Plaudit. Reportedly, he liked Nick the better of the two, so agreed to sell Plaudit.

On the Philmont Ranch, Plaudit earned his keep as a ranch horse, breeding horse, and occasional polo mount. The ranch ran about 3,000 Herefords, plus 9,000 sheep. Although Waite Phillips is deceased, his son, Elliott "Chote" Phillips, remembers the yellow stallion well.

"I rode him quite a bit. He had a lot of speed, and we raced him some. I'll tell you what—any time that horse could get off the mark at the start of a race, he'd definitely win.

"All his colts had speed. We could breed him to a Percheron and get something that

This photo of Plaudit was taken at the Philmont Ranch horse corrals, and the rider is believed to be Tommie Rupert. The date is unknown.

"He was smart, had a good disposition, and was classy looking."

We weren't commercial breeders looking to make a name for ourselves.

"Dad gave most of the ranch to the Boy Scouts of America in 1941. He included Plaudit and the mares, which, to me, was a mistake. They had no use for horses of that caliber, so they wound up selling them."

Many of the mares were purchased by Hank Wiescamp of Alamosa, Colo., and they went on to become foundation mares in Hank's breeding program. Plaudit was sold to Hal Cooper of Oklahoma.

There's no official race record for Plaudit since he never participated in a recognized competition. But he surely left an impressive running record on the New Mexico bush tracks.

It could be that Elliott Phillips is somewhat modest concerning Plaudit's siring accomplishments while at Philmont.

After all, that's where he sired the great running horse Question Mark. He also sired a number of mares who turned out to be great producers. Among them was Miss Helen, the dam of Gold Mount, who went on to sire the legendary Maddon's Bright Eyes. For Hank Wiescamp, Miss Helen produced Skipper's Lad, who became an outstanding sire, and who left his mark in the halter horse world through his son, Skipa Star.

It's not known exactly how long Hal Cooper owned Plaudit before he sold him to Frank Burns of Alamosa, Colo., who was heavily involved in racing. Burns was familiar with the Plaudit horses through his next-door neighbor, Hank Wiescamp. While Burns owned the horse, he sired Scooter W, who was out of a Wiescamp mare, Saucy Sue, by Lani Chief (TB). Foaled in 1945, and owned by Hank, Scooter W won the 1948 World Champion Quarter Running Stallion championship.

But the palomino met up with some bad luck while he was owned by Burns. While in pasture with his mares, Plaudit severely injured a front leg when crossing a creek. He evidently ran the pointed end of a

was fast. He was also smart, had a good disposition, and was classy looking. His offspring had the same qualities," Phillips continued.

"We had about 100 mares back then, and several studs; but Plaudit was the best of them all. We used to buy quite a few mares off the track in Tijuana. Pepito was one of those, and when bred to Plaudit, she produced Question Mark.

"In some ways, I guess Plaudit out-bred himself. I think Plaudit would have gone down as one of the most outstanding sires in history if he'd been in the hands of someone whose intention was to breed him to only the best mares. That wasn't the case with us. We bred horses to use.

Plaudit lived his last 8 years with Mr. and Mrs. Leon Harms, shown here with their daughter, Joan.

Photo Courtesy of Phil Livingston

submerged stump into the leg, which caused a wicked cut. When the horse was found by fishermen several days later, he was in bad shape with a severe infection.

Plaudit was taken to the veterinary school at Colorado A & M (now Colorado State University) in Fort Collins. There, he began a new chapter in his life with two men. One was R.S. Roskelly, Ph.D., a professor at A & M, and the other was a young veterinary student, Robert Poulson, who now lives in Bountiful, Utah. The two knew each other through church affiliations.

Roskelly died in 1991, but his daughter, Suzanne Miller, remembers Plaudit, and says, "Plaudit represented a special era in my dad's life." She relates that Plaudit was at the college about the time her dad decided to buy a horse. He struck a deal with Burns that he would buy Plaudit if the horse could be saved.

Poulson, meanwhile, was a member of the round-the-clock team of students and veterinarians working on Plaudit. He recalls, "The wound was a mess, and I almost flunked out of vet school because I spent so much time with the horse. This happened before we had antibiotics, so we were trying to draw out the infection. We tied a truck inner tube around the leg, filled it with Epsom salts and bran, and kept adding hot water (heated on a hot plate) to that mixture." It was time-

Bob Poulson with Plaudit, when the horse was a patient at Colorado A&M and Bob was a student; spring of 1945.

133

One of Plaudit's most famous sons was Question Mark, shown here at the Tulsa State Fair; the date is unknown. Foaled in 1937, Question Mark—named for his crooked blaze—was out of the Thoroughbred mare Pepito. In his racing prime, he once defeated the famed mare Shue Fly. He passed on his speed to his offspring.

Photo by Paul E. Yard

consuming, but successful.

Roskelly not only bought Plaudit, but also 15 mares from Burns. "Dad had to lease a place to keep them," Suzanne laughs. "The story has come down that Plaudit was no longer able to pasture breed because of the bad leg, but that's not true. He did fine.

"Dad was always telling me how fantastic the horse was . . . that he could sire speed and athletic ability . . . rope horses, cutting horses, anything. He could put speed into anything. One time, Plaudit got out and bred a little black Welsh mare. She had a filly that proved to be one of the fastest mares in the area. I barrel raced on her for years."

Dr. Poulson remembers Plaudit as having "one of the prettiest, kindest eyes I'd ever seen. He was a gold palomino with dapples, stood about 15 hands and weighed around 1,100 pounds. He had

a good back with a powerful loin and hindquarters that carried down into a nice blend with his gaskins. His disposition was excellent. After his injury, he did have a noticeable limp at the trot, but could still get out and run."

When Roskelly took a new job in Pullman, Wash., he took Plaudit with him . . . and later to Utah for several years. "Then Dad was offered an assignment in Iran," says Suzanne. "That's when he sold Plaudit to Leon Harms in New Mexico. It was sad for him, but there was no way he could haul him to Iran."

It was 1950, and the yellow horse was 20 years old. Harms had long admired the stallion, and his primary intention was to make certain he enjoyed the remainder of his life. In 1958, the old injury flared up, the stallion began suffering, and Harms made the difficult decision to put him down.

Plaudit, along with a large slice of yellow horse history, was buried behind Harms' house in Albuquerque.

QUICK M SILVER

22

SOME HORSES are just born tough, and the really tough ones manage to stay that way. At least, that's how it was with a gray ghost named Quick M Silver. He never gave up. He never quit. He was as hard-knocking as they came. He ran, and won, all over the country. It's hard to determine if he logged the most miles on racetracks or in a trailer.

He had powerful hindquarters with heavy muscling in the gaskins, and hocks low to the ground. He put away 75 official races. The last time he heard the call to post was November 21, 1960, when he was 8 years old.

His name was Quick M Silver, and he was a gray bred by Landon K. Moore of Raton, New Mexico. It was 1952 when he took his first gulp of air. His dam was Blue Bonnet Moore by Smokey Moore by Plaudit. And he was sired by Brush Mount by Chimney Sweep (TB). He eventually wound up in Colorado, becoming the pride and joy of Bruce Penley.

"I saw Quick M Silver when he was a big weaner," recalls Penley. "It was 1953 at

He ran, and won, all over the country.

Quick M Silver, a hard-knocking race horse in the 1950s.

Photo by Jack Stribling

135

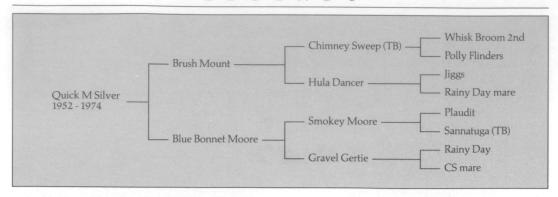

Halter and Performance Record: Starts: 75; 1st: 18, 2nd: 13, 3rd: 13, 4th: 16; total money won: $23,100; Superior Race Horse; Racing Register of Merit.

Progeny Record:

AQHA Champions: 1	Performance Registers of Merit: 5
Foal Crops: 19	Race Money Earned: $165,595
Foals Registered: 261	Race Registers of Merit: 59
Halter-Point Earners: 6	Race Starters: 116
Halter Points Earned: 75	Superior Halter Awards: 1
Performance-Point Earners: 15	Superior Performance Awards: 1
Performance Points Earned: 165	Superior Race Awards: 2
Leading Race Money Earner: Plata Mucho ($19,231)	

the National Western in Denver. I was a cattleman—still am—and my interest was in cutting and reining horses. I'd never given much thought to racing.

"I was looking for a young replacement horse when I first saw Quick M Silver. He had my attention as soon as I saw the muscling in his gaskins."

Penley was definitely attracted to the colt, but he didn't say or do too much until he could look at the long-haired, rough-looking youngster in his stall. No one was around, so Penley took the liberty of opening the door and going in.

"I took him out," admitted Penley. "He responded instantly to any movement. I liked that, and I liked him. I looked at him several more times, and decided I'd be there on sale day. I didn't know if I could afford him, but I intended to try.

"Well, my 'try' wasn't good enough. All the money I had was $300 and it didn't get

him. I left there without him. I got home, and told my wife I'd made the biggest mistake of my life; I'd let the best horse get away from me."

According to Penley, it was somewhere around a year later when he ran into Lawrence Peake, the gentleman who bought Quick M Silver in Denver.

"I asked him what happened to that gray thing he bought in Denver," he laughed. "Peake was really a Thoroughbred man. He told me he got Quick M Silver home, his family came out and looked at the colt, and thought Peake had gone crazy. They didn't like the colt at all.

"Well, I can tell you that hearing him say that was music to my ears. I offered him $375, and he took it."

Quick M Silver found himself at Penley's ranch just south of Denver, near Sedalia, along with a bunch of white-faced cattle.

"I started cutting cattle on him in corrals," recalled Penley. "There was nobody working with me. One day, I put a bunch of yearling calves in a pen—with just me and Quick M Silver. I'd never been able to do that on any other horse because none of them could move that fast. Right then and there, I decided the colt could run."

Once Penley made that decision, there was nothing to do but try.

Quick M Silver was hauled to nearby Centennial Race Track in Littleton for what was destined to be the first of many trips for the heavy-muscled gray stallion. He finished second to Connie Leo in a 350-yard contest. And that was after the green colt was left standing in the gate!

"The mare was no more than a nose in front of him at the wire," laughed Penley. "I asked her owner if we could have an-

Quick M Silver finished third in this race at Los Alamitos in December 1957. The winner (No. 5) was Pap, with Miss Myrna Bar (No. 3) placing second.

All Quick M cared about was running, and he earned a AAA rating.

other go at her, but he refused."

Tom Penley, Bruce's son, was along on all those trips with Quick M Silver and his father. "That horse was broke so good at 3 that he couldn't be ridden like a regular race horse," he explained. "That's what happened to him in his first out at Centennial. He wouldn't run into the bit, so a jockey had to make adjustments.

"His first four races were against lesser-quality horses, but that was it. From then on, he only ran against good ones."

It didn't take long for the gray stallion to learn the racetrack ropes. He didn't care where he was. He didn't care about the name of the track. He didn't care whether the sun was shining or buckets of rain were falling. All Quick M cared about was running, and he earned a AAA rating.

"He reached a point where nothing could beat him out of the gate," said Tom. "He won four of six 440 races. Even so, he developed a reputation for being a short runner. I think one of the reasons

was his speed at the break. He was sure a whale of a horse."

There was a horse by the name of Crocket Jake who had become the deadly scourge of the Colorado bush tracks. Rumor had it Crocket Jake's owner wanted to take a shot at Quick M Silver.

"I got a call one day," remembers Bruce, "asking me to bring Quick M Silver to Durango to run at Crocket Jake. I agreed.

"Well, we didn't always use our horse's right name in the bushes; and Crocket Jake always went by the name of Starvation.

"We stayed outside town when we hit Durango. The day of the race, I loaded Quick M Silver and my jockey and drove to the track. I decided to run Quick M under the name of Hosteen. It's what I used to call my jockey when we were at the ranch.

"Well, you won't believe what happened. We loaded into the gate, and then the others said they weren't going to run because Quick M had a fictitious name. 'Well, what about Starvation?' I asked. There were eight horses in the race and we had to load and unload three times because people kept questioning the fictitious names. I finally told them we were either going to run or forget the whole thing, and I didn't care if Man o' War was in the race. Well, we ran—and we won." Starvation finished second.

Penley and Quick M Silver loaded up again and headed for California. "He took a lot of that California money," chuckled Penley. "He paid his way and mine, too, and all he had in him was oats, hay, and water.

"When we arrived in California, everybody already knew about that race in Durango with ol' Starvation. Our reputation had preceded us, and Quick M already had their respect.

"I'll tell you what, there was one time when I left Los Alamitos with Quick M Silver and Miss Louton in my trailer. I always figured that was one time when I had the two best horses in the country standing behind me. It felt good."

According to Bruce and Tom, the only competitors Quick M Silver never outran were Go Man Go and Vanetta Dee. He was pitted against some of the toughest around, but he always emerged the toughest of them all.

"He was a proud horse," said Penley. "He had calcium deposits in his knees, but no one ever saw him gimp at the track. He would never think about letting anyone see him that way. That, I think, is what we call heart and class.

"Quick M had a great disposition around people, but he changed around other horses. One thing for darned sure . . . he'd always get fighting mad if another horse tried to pass him."

Penley retired Quick M Silver in 1960. His last race was at Los Alamitos where he cracked a sesamoid. He was 8 years old.

Penley stood the gray stallion in Colorado, and then moved him to Norco, Calif., for a while. Then it was back to Colorado.

"We bred a lot of mares to him, and a lot of his babies were gray," said Penley. "He sired some good ones, such as Quick Witch, but I don't think he ever put anything on the ground who could run with him."

However, he did sire a number of offspring who earned their ROM in racing . . . horses like Quick Tex, Miss Penley, Silver Loot, Skyjacker, Shoot M Quick, and Quick O Silver. One of his sons, Highjacker (out of Clara Decker), became an AQHA Champion.

Penley adds, "Quick M Silver was tough as nails and about as fast as lightning. He put both those qualities in his offspring. Most of them were on the small side, but so darned quick they could jump right out from under a rider.

"In my book, Quick M was one of the greats."

The tough gray horse who was his owner's pride and joy died at the age of 22. He was buried at Penley's ranch.

Author's note: Since this interview in 1992, Bruce Penley passed away—on February 20, 1993.

"Quick M Silver was tough as nails and about as fast as lightning."

Star Duster

23

MANY PEDIGREES still carry the name Star Duster, a sorrel stallion bred by Fred Lowry of Lenapah, Oklahoma. Foaled in 1944, he was by Nowata Star by Oklahoma Star, and out of Lowry's Mabel.

Although it was Leonard Milligan who brought Star Duster from Oklahoma to Colorado, it was Quentin Semotan of Steamboat Springs, Colo., who put the stallion on the map.

"Star Duster was a yearling when I first saw him," says Semotan. "Leonard (Milligan) showed him at the Denver Stock Show and he won his class. I'd been looking for a horse to buy, and I had certain things in mind. I wanted a heavy-muscled individual, and nothing I'd seen suited me—until I saw Star Duster.

"There wasn't an ounce of fat on him. Just good muscle on good conformation standing on good legs."

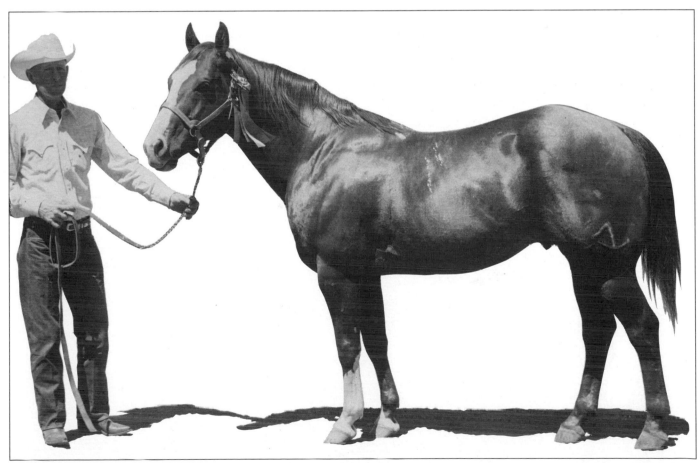

Star Duster and Quentin Semotan at the Laramie (Wyo.) Jubilee Quarter Horse Show in 1955, where Star Duster won the aged stallion class and was named grand champion stallion.
Photo by James Cathey

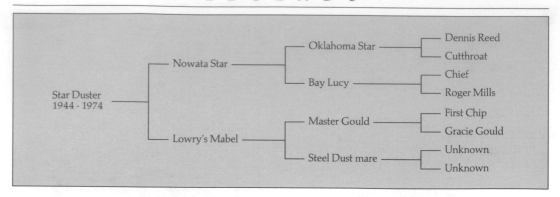

				Dennis Reed
			Oklahoma Star	Cutthroat
	Nowata Star			Chief
Star Duster			Bay Lucy	Roger Mills
1944 - 1974			Master Gould	First Chip
	Lowry's Mabel			Gracie Gould
			Steel Dust mare	Unknown
				Unknown

Halter and Performance Record: 1 Halter Point.

Progeny Record:

AQHA Champions: 5	Performance Points Earned: 276
Foal Crops: 29	Performance Registers of Merit: 14
Foals Registered: 434	Race Money Earned: $4,846
Halter-Point Earners: 50	Race Registers of Merit: 5
Halter Points Earned: 471	Superior Halter Awards: 2
Performance-Point Earners: 26	

Leading Race Money Earner: Twinkle Duster ($1,505)

This photo may have been taken when Star Duster won the champion of champions title at Fort Worth in 1948. **Photo by James Cathey**

"Even today, Star Duster would be considered as having good conformation. He was a sorrel with a blaze, stocking on the left front leg, and a partial sock on the right front. He stood 14.3 and weighed just a hair over 1,200. There wasn't an ounce of fat on him. Just good muscle on good conformation standing on good legs."

Semotan and Milligan got together and struck a deal on Star Duster. "I started showing him," continued Semotan. "We won at the Colorado State Fair. We went back to Denver's National Western Stock Show and wound up in the same class of 3-year-olds as Poco Bueno, owned by E. Paul Waggoner. We took reserve champion in that one. We stood grand champion the next year (1948) at Denver."

Semotan can't hold back a chuckle as he remembers this part of his Star Duster story. "Mr. Waggoner was at Denver when we went back and took grand. Afterwards, he told me he'd bet $500 he could beat me in Fort Worth. Well, $500 was a lot of money. I had all the confidence in the world in Star Duster, but I didn't bet. We did go to Fort Worth, though, and ended up champion of champions."

These wins, however, are not reflected in Star Duster's AQHA record because in those days, records were handwritten; record-keeping was not as accurate as it is now, and later, when the association switched to computers, some of the information was possibly lost.

Semotan bought Star Duster first and foremost for the stallion's conformation. Apparently, a lot of arena judges agreed with the Colorado cattleman's preference. The pair became a familiar sight in Denver, Chicago, and California.

"I helped start the Rocky Mountain Quarter Horse Association," explained Semotan. "I had Star Duster colts in our first sale, and topped the sale more than once. My colts were never slick and shiny because the sale was in the winter; but I always fed good, so they were fat." Semotan's livelihood came from cattle, something he learned from his father who moved from Iowa to homestead in Colorado. His love for horses, though, was always in the forefront.

"I used to buy a few, sell a few, make a little money here and there," reminisced Semotan. "I bred quite a few mares to Star Duster, but we were so far away from everyone that it was hard to get a lot of outside mares to him. At one time, I had about 100 head of horses with a lot of mares from the Peter McCue line. Star Duster crossed extremely well on those."

What Semotan had in Star Duster was one horse who could do a lot of things well. He excelled when it came to halter. "We could also do anything on him," he says. "I never did race him officially, but

Evelyn Semotan, Quentin's wife, aboard Star Duster in 1952.

A 1948 photo of Star Duster and Quentin Semotan, probably taken at Denver.

Photo by Simsick

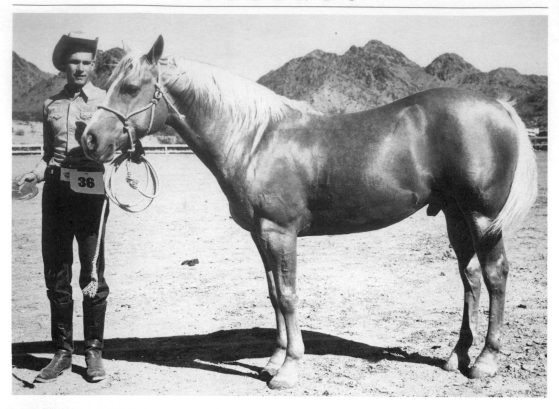

One of Star Duster's better-known sons was G Fern Hornet, a palomino stallion out of Laura's Panzarita (by Ding Bob), foaled in 1948. This picture was taken at the 1954 Arizona Palomino Show in Phoenix, where Hornet won several classes and was named grand champion stallion. He was bred by Semotan, but owned by Mrs. Gayle Jennings of Scottsdale, and was shown by her son, Gayle Jennings Jr.

Photo by Charlie Ray

Barbara Star, a daughter of Star Duster foaled in 1948, was the AQHA Honor Roll Halter Horse in 1956. She was owned by R.Q. Sutherland of Kansas City.

Steen, a good son of Star Duster foaled in 1954, was an AQHA Champion.

I did a fair amount of matching with friends.

"I worked cattle on Star Duster. I also roped off him, and not one time did that horse break a barrier. Not once. He was fast, athletic, smart, and well-mannered."

The horse who did everything for Semotan also sired outstanding sons and daughters, and he became a leading maternal grandsire of AQHA Champions (13). He sired five race ROMs, and one of those, Cowboy 2 Duster, was also a Superior Halter Horse. Barbara Star was the 1956 AQHA high-point halter horse, and produced (by Skipper's King) AQHA Champion Skip A Barb.

"You can look at pedigrees today and see horses who trace to him," mused Semotan with pride. "He was outstanding. I kept him until he was 13. Then I traded him to J. Ralph Bell. He ended up in Idaho with Thane Lancaster, and died sometime in his 30s. I'll say one thing . . . he sure gave everything he had for as long as he had it."

142

JOE REED P-3 was the result of an unplanned breeding between a swift Louisiana mare known as Della Moore and a royally bred Thoroughbred named Joe Blair. Even though his breeding was unintentional, he was destined for greatness.

Without Joe Reed, the Quarter Horse industry would not have had Joe Reed II, Leo, Joak, Red Joe of Arizona, and others who have sired so many outstanding horses. And his greatness passed down through succeeding generations. Take Red Joe of Arizona, for example. He sired the mare named Ready, who became the dam of Barred, who sired Miss Night Bar, who in turn produced Jet Deck, who sired Easy Jet. But we are getting ahead of the story.

Joe Reed's dam, Della Moore, was bred by Ludovic Stemmans of Lafayette, Louisiana. She was by Old D.J. (Dedier), a darn good match race horse who later gained more fame as a producer of broodmares.

As there is with the pedigrees of so many other early-day horses, there is confusion regarding Della Moore's dam. The AQHA lists her dam as La Hernandez, yet several reliable writers of Quarter Horse history, including Bob Denhardt, have written that her dam was Belle, by Sam Rock, a noted speedburner. This is probably incorrect.

The original listing for the second dam of Joe Reed in AQHA Studbook No. 2 was "Hernandez mare by Dewey," and this information probably came direct from his registration application. This was later changed to La Hernandez.

In his excellent book, *Cajun-Bred Running Horses*, F.S. LeBlanc expounded a bit further: "Della Moore's dam was owned by Antoine Hernandez of Scott (who gave his name to La Hernandez)." One authority says that the early Cajuns were a tight-knit group with a suspicious eye toward strangers, and possibly they did not give correct information to Bob Denhardt.

There is no disputing, however, that Della Moore became a terrific race mare. Her ownership also passed from Stemmans to Demontan Broussard to Boyd Simar. Then when she was around 8 years old, Simar sold her to Henry Lindsey of Granger, Texas. By then, Della was considered virtually unbeatable, and so Simar would sometimes lease the mare back for

Even though his breeding was unintentional, he was destined for greatness.

Old Joe Reed at 27 years.

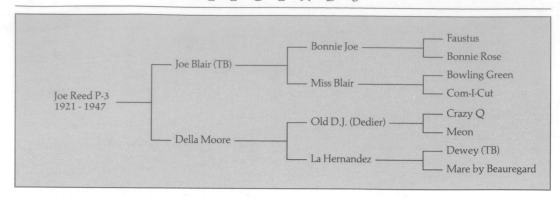

Halter and Performance Record: None.

Progeny Record:

Foal Crops: 18
Foals Registered: 184
Halter-Point Earners: 8
Halter Points Earned: 25
Performance-Point Earners: 2
Performance Points Earned: 224
Leading Race Money Earner: Jupiter Joe ($3,881)

Performance Registers of Merit: 1
Race Money Earned: $4,424
Race Registers of Merit: 6
Race Starters: 13
Superior Performance Awards: 1
World Champions (Racing): 1

A photo of Joe Reed after Dr. Slankard bought him in the late 1930s. Possibly that's Dr. Slankard leading him. **Photo Courtesy of Jim Norton**

certain races. One of those took place during a San Antonio meet in either 1919 or 1920.

It was springtime, and she was stalled next to an extremely well-bred Thoroughbred stallion, Joe Blair, one of the fastest sprinters of that era. As the oft-told story goes, one night when Della was in season, she and Joe Blair were raising a terrible ruckus while some of the stable hands were shooting craps. They finally got so tired of all the noise the two equine love-birds were making that they put the two together.

Another version of this tale says that both horses were being rested between races at a nearby ranch when the breeding took place. Whichever version is true, apparently no one told anybody about it.

After the San Antonio meet, Simar returned Della to Lindsey and never mentioned that the mare might be in foal, possibly because he didn't know. Some months later, however, Della's trainer was certainly puzzled when the mare wouldn't "draw down," even though he kept cutting back on her feed.

The mare subsequently foaled a stocking-legged sorrel colt, later named Joe Reed. The AQHA recognizes his official foaling year of birth as 1921, but many old-timers contend that he was actually foaled in 1920 and was a year older than he was supposed to be. What is known for sure is that the colt was small—some said he was stunted—because his dam had not been well fed.

Lindsey's main concern was to wean the sorrel colt as soon as possible. He did just that when Joe Reed was a scant 3 months

The QUARTER HORSE

Vol. 2 - No. 7   **KNOX CITY, TEXAS**   OCTOBER - 1947

Subscription price: $2 per year   All contents copyrighted 1947   Single copies 25c

Official Publication of

THE NATIONAL QUARTER HORSE BREEDERS ASSOCIATION

R. J. (Rusty) Bradley, Jr., *President*   Ed Bateman, Sr., *Editor*   J. M. Huffington, *Sec'y-Treas.*

The cover of the October 1947 issue of The Quarter Horse, which was the official publication of The National Quarter Horse Breeders Association, featured Joe Reed P-3.

Oklahoma Founding Sire Had Great Breeding Career

JOE REED—His Sons and Daughters Carry On the Fine Speed and Power of His Notable Blood Lines — Read His Story In This Issue.

The colt was small—some said he was stunted—because his dam had not been well fed.

Entered as Second Class matter at the postoffice at Knox City, Texas, under Act of March 3, 1879. Published monthly. Business address of The QUARTER HORSE is Box 547, Knox City, Texas; Telephone 3102. While exercising reasonable care, the publishers will not be responsible for the safe return of unsolicited manuscripts or photographs sent in for publication. STAFF: DALE GRAHAM, Associate Editor; Photographers, Tommy Thompson, 112 S. Washington, San Angelo, Texas, specialist in livestock photography and photo-finish; BILLIE WILCOX, Box 333, Olympia, Washington, specialist in photo-finish. Editorial contributors, DANA STONER, Houston; NELSON C. NYE, Tucson, Ariz.; MRS. LUTHER BULLOCK, Texola, Oklahoma. The National Quarter Horse Breeders Association hereby gives notice that it reserves the right in case of any dispute over subscription rates and changes in said rates, made with or without notice, to return any sum already paid in, or proffered it, for subscribing to The QUARTER HORSE. ADVERTISING RATES: full page $60; half page $30; one-third page $20; inch rate $2.00, with minimum size of 4 inches. Standard breeder ad on yearly contract only. $6 per month or $66 per year. No classified ads accepted. Engravings 65 to 85 screen. Copy deadline, receipt of same in QUARTER HORSE office by 25th of month preceding publication. Contracts: rate open only and subject to change by notification after any date of issue.

old, putting him on cow's milk and returning Della to training. For the most part, Joe Reed was left to himself, running in pasture and collecting burs in his mane and tail. Lindsey had little use for a colt with an unknown sire.

It was at least a year later when Lindsey learned the name of the sire. Lindsey couldn't have done better had he planned the breeding himself.

Bred by Charles B. Campbell of Minco,

Okla., Joe Blair was a Thoroughbred who didn't fit the conventional mold of his breed. Foaled in 1911, he hit the match tracks and soon made it clear he was far more talented at shorter distances than he was in longer, more typical Thoroughbred races.

Joe Blair's breeding was certainly no

Joe Sunday was considered one of Joe Reed's better sons. He was foaled in 1941, and this photo was taken at the 1953 Colorado Springs show where he won the aged stallion class. According to his AQHA record, this was the only time he was ever shown. He was owned by M.R. Harrison of Rocky Ford, Colorado.

Della Moore. After she produced Joe Reed, Henry Lindsey sold her to Ott Adams of Alice, Tex., for whom she produced Joe Moore and Grano de Oro. Joe Moore—by Little Joe by Traveler—became a leading maternal grandsire of ROM race colts.

accident. Campbell was financially comfortable, and used at least a portion of his money to acquire several hundred high-quality broodmares. His breeding program was noted for some of the finest sprinting blood of the day, including Bonnie Joe (Joe Blair's sire) and Bowling Green, who was the sire of Miss Blair, Joe Blair's dam.

Joe Blair was a sprinter with blazing speed. Bert Wood of Arizona, who later purchased Joe Reed II, was one of the stallion's early handlers. "Joe Blair wasn't very big," recalled Wood, "but he was beautiful. He didn't run the longer Thoroughbred distances. His best lick was at the shorter ones. I exercised him, and liked him from the first time I touched him. I would have bought him if I'd had the money."

When Henry Lindsey learned of Joe Reed's highly respectable sire, he brought the half-starved colt into the barn, pulled out the burs, poured feed to him, and had him ready to run by the time he was a 2-year-old in 1923. By then, Lindsey had sold Della Moore to the renowned Ott Adams of Alice, Texas.

Joe Reed definitely responded to the attention heaped on him, but his lack of early proper nourishment had taken its

Red Joe of Arizona, one of Joe Reed's best sons, as pictured in AQHA's Studbook No. 3. He was owned by Mr. and Mrs. Hewitt Wagner of Winkelman, Arizona.

toll. He was small, and certainly didn't turn any heads when Lindsey took him, along with the rest of his string, to the track in Omaha, Nebraska. The attitudes changed, however, when the little sorrel stud hit the 16th pole in 5.4 one morning in a workout.

Joe Reed was lightning fast, just like his sire and dam. Still, though, he was fast during the era when Thoroughbreds and longer distances were the dominant forces in racing. "Short" horses had to race at the brush tracks.

Lindsey sold the sorrel with the four white socks in 1924 to Harve Dennison, who then sold him to J.W. House of Cameron, Texas. He was a coming 5-year-old at the time of that sale. House owned him for a number of years, and the horse ran many a race. No records are available as to the number of races he won, but it's been written that at the quarter-mile, he was tough to beat.

In the June 1948 issue of *The Quarter Horse*, House was quoted: "I never saw Joe start with a bunch of horses that he didn't get right out in front and leave them on the jump. He had so much power when

READY #1493, CAQRH

This ad, picturing Ready, also appeared in AQHA's Studbook No. 3. The mare shown, Ready, was by Red Joe of Arizona. When bred to Three Bars (TB), she produced Barred.

he started that he would spread his plates. He nearly crippled himself in this manner, and we were finally forced to shoe him with a bar across the heel."

When House retired the horse from the track, he began breeding him. In Nelson Nye's article about Joe Reed in the October 1947 issue of *The Quarter Horse*, House was quoted as follows:

"I bred him to the mares around

147

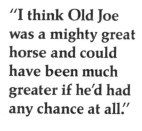

Catechu, out of Diamond Oakes, by A.D. Reed by Peter McCue, was one of Joe Reed's best sons and a leading maternal grandsire of ROM race colts.

Photo Courtesy of Phil Livingston

"I think Old Joe was a mighty great horse and could have been much greater if he'd had any chance at all."

here. Most of them didn't have no breeding at all, but every colt could run, and some of them pretty fast. I had two good mares, Little Red Nell and Nellene. I raised Red Joe of Arizona from Red Nell and Joe Reed II out of Nellene. I never saw a sorry horse by Joe Reed, no matter how sorry the mare."

Joe Reed II was foaled in 1938, and House sold Old Joe Reed to Jesse J. Slankard, D.V.M. of Elk City, Okla., about the same time. Slankard kept the horse for the rest of his life.

In the same article mentioned earlier, Nye quotes Slankard as saying, "Joe had a world of good sense. . . . I think Old Joe was a mighty great horse and could have been much greater if he'd had any chance at all."

Slankard also told about the time "the boys" wanted to rope calves on Old Joe, but he warned them Joe would be too fast. Sure enough, they had to try it, and

when Joe broke out of the box, he shot right by the calf before his rider could even swing a loop.

In a 1960 issue of *The Quarter Horse Journal,* Franklin Reynolds wrote the following about Joe Reed: "In his prime, Joe Reed stood about 14.2 and weighed just about 1,000 pounds when in good condition. He had a blaze and four socks. His neck was, some people thought, a trifle long. His ears were small, and his head was small and very shapely. His gaskin was good and he was unusually well-muscled inside the foreleg. Even as an aged horse, he was always 'on center' with his legs well-gathered under him."

Joe Reed P-3 died of a heart attack on May 17, 1947. In addition to horses already mentioned, some of his best-known offspring included Little Fanny, Reed McCue, Joe Sunday, Joe Bob, Sue Reed, Joe Darter, and Catechu.

When the AQHA was formed, Joe Reed was given the number P-3, designating him as one of the breed's most important foundation sires.

148

JOE REED II

JOE REED II proved that he not only had speed, being named the Champion Quarter Running Stallion in 1942-43, but also a heart as big as all outdoors. During his brief racing career, he ran on a badly injured foot. Let's look at his background first, however.

He was bred by J.W. House of Cameron, Tex., who owned Joe Reed P-3. House had raced Old Joe, and was duly impressed by his speed; but what House really wanted

was a stud horse. He figured the best way to find out the stallion's potential as a sire was to breed him to the best mare he owned. That turned out to be Nellene. (No one is absolutely certain, but it's said Nellene ran her last race when she was 6 months in foal with Joe Reed II.)

Nellene's sire was the sprinting Thoroughbred named Fleeting Time, who was by High Time by Ultimus, who was a double-bred Domino. Many horsemen

"Some horses are born to run and Joe Reed II was one of those."

Joe Reed II was not only a top race horse, but also a halter winner.

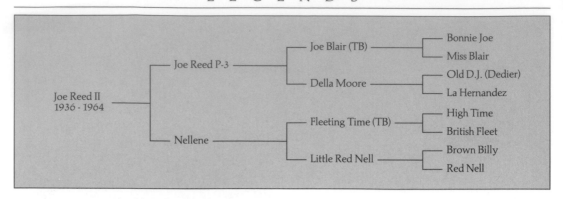

```
                                              ┌─── Bonnie Joe
                           ┌── Joe Blair (TB) ─┤
                           │                   └─── Miss Blair
            ┌── Joe Reed P-3 ─┤
            │              │                   ┌─── Old D.J. (Dedier)
            │              └── Della Moore ────┤
Joe Reed II ─┤                                 └─── La Hernandez
1936 - 1964 │
            │                                   ┌─── High Time
            │              ┌── Fleeting Time (TB) ─┤
            │              │                    └─── British Fleet
            └── Nellene ───┤
                           │                    ┌─── Brown Billy
                           └── Little Red Nell ──┤
                                                └─── Red Nell
```

Halter and Performance Record: 1942-43 World Champion Quarter Running Stallion.

Progeny Record:

AQHA Champions: 1	Performance Points Earned: 79
Foal Crops: 25	Performance Registers of Merit: 4
Foals Registered: 347	Race Money Earned: $271,330
Halter-Point Earners: 9	Race Registers of Merit: 66
Halter Points Earned: 49	Race Starters: 144
Performance-Point Earners: 9	Superior Race Awards: 6
Leading Race Money Earner: Tonta Lad ($30,542)	

of that era felt there was no better blood than that of Domino. Nellene was out of Little Red Nell by Brown Billy—more good breeding.

Joe Reed II hit the ground in 1936. House stood back and assessed him with the eye of an artist looking at a valuable painting. He could find the colt lacking in no way, shape, or form. He was so confident that Joe Reed II would be the sire he dreamed of having that he started breeding him before breaking him. He exhibited his confidence again when he sold Joe Reed P-3. After all, he had the son, and the son appeared to be better than the father.

But in 1941, Bert Wood of Tucson, Ariz., convinced House to sell Joe Reed II to him.

Just thinking about it, most people would assume Wood wanted Joe Reed II as a breeding stallion. After all, he was coming 5 and had never been ridden. Due to a

barbed wire injury while he was owned by House, he was also crippled with a left knee that was chronically swollen and stiff. But . . . no . . . Wood wanted to race the horse!

"Well, I was looking for a stallion, too," said Wood, "but I needed to find out whether or not he could run before I could expect people to send mares to him.

"I was convinced he had speed. When I was just a kid, I exercised Joe Blair (Joe Reed's sire) while he was at Hayes Ranch in Globe, Arizona. I wasn't any more than a big kid then, living with my folks who'd moved to Arizona from Texas. Dad had a ranch at El Capitan, and horses were part of everything. Anyway, I was always impressed with Joe Blair and I never forgot him.

"I'd never seen Joe Reed P-3, but I sure knew about him. As a matter of fact, I didn't see him until he was an older horse in Oklahoma. He was big, refined, and good-looking."

Wood contacted House and set up a time to visit. House led out Joe Reed II. "I thought he was the best horse I'd ever seen in my life," recalled Wood more than 50 years later. "He was absolutely beautiful. Perfectly made. Beautiful head. Perfect disposition. His left knee was in bad shape, but I never saw him give to it. He was too proud for that. I paid House $500 for him and brought him to Arizona."

Wood was determined to race Joe Reed II. But first he had to get him broke, which House had never bothered to do. Wood was ranching then, so he broke Joe as a ranch

This 1943 photo of Joe Reed II appeared in The Quarter Horse *(April 1949), which was published by The National Quarter Horse Breeders Association.*

horse and used him a bunch to work cattle. He says Joe was smart, and learned fast.

During the winter of 1942-43, Wood made up his mind to go ahead and race Joe, even though he had not been able to teach the horse anything about racing. Then, bad luck. While following a cow up a dry sand wash one day, Joe stepped on a broken bottle. "It was an awfully bad cut on his right front foot," said Wood. The cut resulted in a quarter crack that never completely healed.

Even though Joe was 7 and crippled, Wood still had faith in him . . . and wanted to see how he'd get along on the racetrack.

A track called Hacienda Moltacqua had opened at Tucson, and the Tucson Speed Trials were scheduled in February 1943. Wood entered Joe in a Class B race, which attracted a six-horse field, with the favorite being Brown Deacon.

Putting Joe into this race required a large measure of confidence and courage. The stallion had absolutely no race training. He'd never seen a starting gate. He didn't know what it meant to run on a straightaway.

"Some horses are born to run," insisted Wood. "Joe Reed II was one of those. It didn't matter how old he was or how crippled. He did what he'd been born to do."

The gates opened and Joe stood there. The rest of the field had at least 6 lengths

Poison Ivy, a 1944 daughter of Joe Reed II in the winner's circle at Rillito, in Tucson, after winning a 350-yard race in March 1953. She was owned and trained by Bert Wood, who is holding her. That's Dorothy Wood on the left, jockey Jim Curry and Roger Wood mounted, and Vivian Kirk on the right.
Photo Courtesy of Bert and Dorothy Wood

Little Sister W, a daughter of Joe Reed II and a full sister to the immortal Leo. Foaled in 1946, Little Sister W was a black mare. This photo was taken in January 1953, when she won a 400-yard race in 20.8 seconds. Jockeyed by D. Clark, she was owned and trained by Bert Wood, who also bred her. Those shown include Wood (behind the mare), Pokey Clark, and Feral Kent.

Photo Courtesy of Bert and Dorothy Wood

on him before his jockey could get him in gear. The crippled stallion found his stride and headed for the finish that was 440 yards away, getting there before anyone else with a half-length to spare.

The crowd at Moltacqua went absolutely wild. They wanted to see more. The stallion had won their hearts and their imaginations. They didn't wait long for an encore performance. It came 7 days later on Valentine's Day.

Wood kept Joe in his stall most of the week between the two races, trying to take care of his bad foot. In the field was some real competition: Chicaro, Arizona Girl, Red Racer, Pay Dirt, and Domino. This time, he broke well and won by 2 full lengths.

One week later, on February 21, Joe Reed II went to the post for his third and last race. It was the open championship for stallions. The distance was 440 yards. Again, Wood had done little with him between races in order to protect his foot. This time, his competition included the famous "Iron Horse," Clabber.

Joe loaded into the 6-hole. Clabber was

Here's another daughter of Joe Reed II, Whisper W. Foaled in 1944, she was bred by Ed Henry and owned by Ed Piggott Jr., both of Tucson. This picture was taken in Tucson in November 1949, when Whisper W won a 220-yarder in 12.5.

Photo Courtesy of Bert and Dorothy Wood

in the 3. The signal came, and Joe and Clabber left heads up with one another. Reports said Clabber unintentionally swerved and hit Joe Reed II a tremendous lick. Both stallions were big, and the impact was strong. But Joe gathered himself up and headed for the finish.

Even today, the few people who are still around who saw that race describe it with a catch of excitement in their voices. The two big stallions tore down the track against a strong head wind, and Joe's nose was in front as they flashed across the finish line.

During the race, however, Joe's bad foot broke open and bled badly, and Wood had to retire him from the track. But, he had found that his horse could run. And as a result of those three sensational victories, Joe was named Champion Quarter Running Stallion of 1942-43.

Bert Wood had tremendous affection for Joe Reed II. Some people might question that statement, asking why he ran the crippled stallion if he thought so highly of him.

"Because, like I said, he was born to run. I knew from the very beginning he could run, but I didn't know how fast he was. I wanted to prove it to me and to everyone else who questioned him."

So why, after that first triumph, did Wood elect to put the stallion back on the track the second and third times? "Those races proved to everyone the first one wasn't an accident. That horse was a combination of two things—tremendous speed and tremendous heart. I think we're only allowed to have one like him in an entire lifetime."

Although his third race marked the end of Joe Reed's racing career, he was later shown in halter classes. His record with AQHA does not reflect this, but at that time, many horses being shown did not

"That horse was a combination of two things— tremendous speed and tremendous heart."

Joak, one of the better sons of Joe Reed II. This picture is from a painting of Joak done in 1967 by Joel Hefley of Colorado Springs.

Leo and a AAA stakes winner; and Joak out of Navie Girl by Cowboy P-12. Joak was AAA, and became a leading maternal grandsire of ROM race colts. When bred to the great racing mare Queenie, Joe Reed II sired Joe Queen, a AAA stakes winner (and whose picture appears in the chapter on Queenie).

Other Joe Reed II foals included Tonta Lad, Sierra Hotshot, Brevity Joe, Mr Joe Big, Sierra Snowman, and Jody B Reed—all rated AAA.

Joe Reed II went on to become a leading sire, and maternal grandsire, of ROM race colts; and a leading maternal grandsire of AQHA Champions.

Bert and Dorothy Wood remember Joe Reed as being a big pet. Wood says, "He helped to raise our kids, and he sure as heck taught them to ride. They used to climb on the fence and then ease on to Joe's back. He just stood there. That horse was something special."

In 1959, Bert and Dorothy decided to get back into cattle ranching, after primarily being in the horse breeding business for a number of years. They sold their place near Tucson, and bought a ranch at Camp Verde, Arizona.

As Dorothy says, "You can't breed horses and raise cattle, and do a good job at both." So Bert reluctantly agreed to let Clarence Lindsey of Bountiful, Utah, take the horse. Lindsey had gone to the Woods' place to look at Joe Reed II colts, and ended up taking the "old man" to his ranch, located at Fort Bridger, Wyoming.

Lindsey's son, Clarence Jr., says that at that time, his dad ran over a hundred broodmares, and got several foal crops by Joe Reed II before the horse died in 1964. Lindsey believes that the horse was buried on his dad's ranch.

have any points recorded with the fledgling association. At Tucson, he twice won the heavyweight stallion class, and in 1944 was grand champion cow horse. Those were halter class titles in those days. Wood's wife, Dorothy, says that Bert could not show the horse under saddle because of Joe's bad foot.

But meantime, Wood was also breeding the horse, and his reputation continued to grow. By 1947, Wood was breeding Joe to as many mares as he could handle, for a fee of $100.

Few horsemen would deny that Leo was Joe Reed II's greatest son, and Leo is discussed in the next chapter. But Joe Reed II also sired Little Sister W, a full sister to

LEO FIRST carved his niche in the early years of the Quarter Horse industry as a sizzling speed horse. But then he cemented his reputation by becoming one of the all-time great sires. While he is recognized primarily as a leading broodmare sire, both his sons and daughters excelled on the track and in the show ring.

Just a few of his outstanding daughters included Miss Meyers, AAAT and the 1953 World Champion Quarter Running Mare and Horse; Mona Leta, Bobbie Leo, Miss Olene, Lady Bird Leo, and Quincy Leota, all AAAT; Leolita and Leola, AAA and AQHA Champions; South Pacific, Rosa Leo, and Garrett's Miss Pawhuska, all outstanding producers of running horses.

The achievements of Leo's sons were pretty shiney, too. Some of the better known include Palleo Pete, AAAT and 1954 Champion Quarter Running Stallion; Leo Tag, AAA and AQHA Champion;

He was a speed horse and one of the all-time great sires.

Leo, one of the greatest broodmare sires in the history of the breed. There is no date on this picture, but it was evidently taken when Leo had some age on him. Leo stood 14.2 and weighed about 1,100 pounds.

Photo Courtesy of Phil Livingston

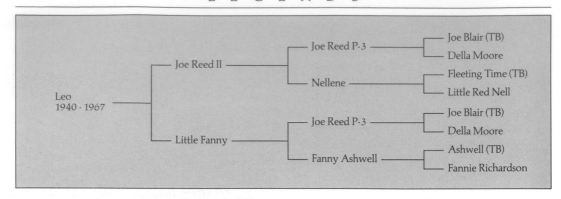

```
                                                    ┌─── Joe Blair (TB)
                              ┌─── Joe Reed P-3 ─────┤
                              │                      └─── Della Moore
              ┌─── Joe Reed II ┤
              │               │                      ┌─── Fleeting Time (TB)
              │               └─── Nellene ──────────┤
   Leo ───────┤                                      └─── Little Red Nell
   1940 - 1967│
              │                                      ┌─── Joe Blair (TB)
              │               ┌─── Joe Reed P-3 ─────┤
              │               │                      └─── Della Moore
              └─── Little Fanny┤
                              │                      ┌─── Ashwell (TB)
                              └─── Fanny Ashwell ────┤
                                                     └─── Fannie Richardson
```

Halter and Performance Record: Racing ROM.

Progeny Record:

AQHA Champions: 24	Race Money Earned: $605,882
Foal Crops: 24	Race Registers of Merit: 211
Foals Registered: 554	Race Starters: 370
Halter-Point Earners: 69	Superior Halter Awards: 4
Halter Points Earned: 935	Superior Performance Awards: 2
Performance-Point Earners: 46	Superior Race Awards: 8
Performance Points Earned: 840.5	Supreme Champions: 1
Performance Registers of Merit: 33	World Champions (Racing): 4
Leading Race Money Earner: Miss Olene ($31,532)	

Leo sired athletic ability as well as speed.

Orren Mixer's well-known painting of Leo. It was on the September 1951 cover of Western Horseman.

Okie Leo, AQHA Champion; Robin Reed, AAAT; Croton Oil, AA and a leading sire of ROM race colts; Leo San, a leading sire of AQHA Champions; and Holey Sox, AA on the track and also the 1963 NCHA World Champion Cutting Horse.

A look at the titles won by Leo's offspring shows that he sired athletic ability as well as speed, and these traits were passed down to succeeding generations. Leo San, for example, became a leading sire of AQHA Champions and sired both Peppy San and Mr San Peppy. Peppy San was NCHA World Champion Cutting Horse in 1967, and Mr San Peppy won the same title in 1974. And both also became outstanding sires of cutting horses. Many of Leo's daughters also became extraordinary producers.

Leo, himself, had a world of speed, and a look at his pedigree shows why. He was a double-bred Joe Reed P-3, since both his sire and dam were by that remarkable horse. That same cross also made him a double-bred Della Moore, one of the greatest racing mares of her era.

Leo's dam, Little Fanny, also had a world of speed in her pedigree, especially on her maternal side. She, herself, was raced twice as a 2-year-old at the quarter mile, and won both starts. Her dam, Fannie Ashwell, was a half-Thoroughbred out of Fannie Richardson, a tremendous sprinter. And Fannie Richardson's dam, Sister Fanny, reportedly won 82 of 85 races.

Little Fanny raced only twice; afterward, she became a broodmare, which is where she made her greatest mark. When bred to Joe Reed II, she not only produced Leo, but also Little Sister W, rated AAA, and Firebrand Reed and Fanny's Finale, both AA. She also produced several other good foals.

Leo was her first foal, and he was bred by John W. House of Cameron, Texas. House, of course, also owned Joe Reed II before selling him to Bert Wood of Tucson. House also sold Little Fanny to Wood, apparently after she produced Leo. In an interview in *The Quarter Horse* (April 1949), published by The National Quarter Horse Breeders Association, House was asked his formula for producing such speed horses as Joe Reed II, Leo, Nellene, and others. His reply:

"Just pick out a proven fast stallion and breed him to a fast mare. Too many of today's breeders think one or the other can do it all, but to get a really top horse, you have to have speed on both sides. Breed up, not down. Everybody that bred to old Joe (Joe Reed P-3) thought they had a race horse, but the ones that bred no-account mares soon found out different, although all of his colts could run fair. You can take speed out of a bloodline faster than you can put it in, and that's what a lot of fellows are doing now."

When Leo was in his 2-year-old year, House sold him to Lester Manning, who ran the sorrel colt at Eagle Pass., Tex., when he was only 18 months old. He ran second against some good competition—and attracted the attention of John W. Tillman of Pawhuska, Okla., who bought the sorrel for a reported $750. While Tillman owned him, Leo won a number of races. Records indicate that at Eagle Pass in 1944, he ran 300 yards in 16.5 seconds, a record at the time. At Pawhuska, also in 1944, he set a track record for 300 yards in 16 flat.

By the time Leo was 3, it was impossible to find anyone to match him against in the Southwest. He also began changing ownership with such rapidity that it is impossible to trace his various sales, and to determine exactly who owned him at what time. It is known, however, that E.M. Salinas of Eagle Pass bought him at one point, and sent him across the border into Mexico for match races. However, a trailer accident resulted in injuries to both of Leo's front legs, and left him with a left knee that was permanently big and misshapen.

Leo was returned to Oklahoma, when owned by W.C. Rowe. But then Rowe, before too long, shipped Leo by train to New Mexico where he was starting a new

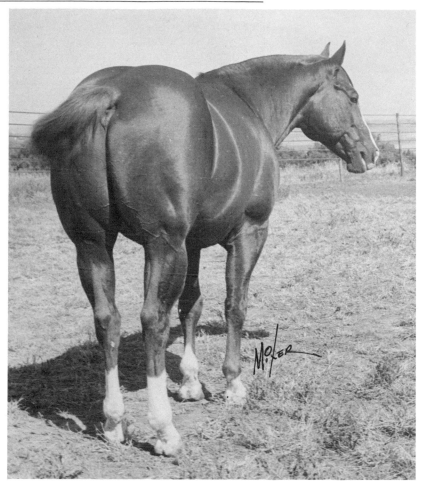

This photo shows the hindquarters that jet-propelled Leo down the tracks.
Photo by Orren Mixer

Little Fanny, Leo's dam, as pictured in The Quarter Horse, June 1948.

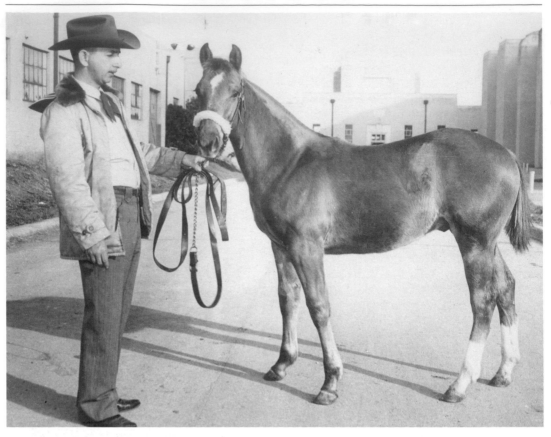

This little guy is Lemac, a 1949 son of Leo and Sorrel Sue, by King. The picture was taken at the 1950 Fort Worth Fat Stock Show, where Bud Warren showed him to first in the yearling stallion class. Lemac went on to sire Leolark, an AQHA Champion who sired Alisa Lark, who in turn produced Rugged Lark, twice the Superhorse at the AQHA World Show (1986 and '88).

**Photo by
Skeet Richardson**

The city of Perry, Okla., in appreciation for all the business that Leo brought to the area, named a city park in his honor, and erected a statue. That's Noble County Extension Director Bob Farabough on the left, and Bud Warren on the right.

ranching operation. As the oft-told story goes, the boxcar containing Leo was lost enroute, and when it was found, Leo was in critical physical condition. He was nursed back to health, however, and sold again . . . this time to Gene Moore of the Rocking M Ranch, Fairfax, Oklahoma.

According to Nelson C. Nye, in his book, *Outstanding Modern Quarter Horse Sires,* Leo ran his last race in Tulsa in the spring of 1947. It was a match race against a horse called Little Joe for a purse of $1,000—at a distance of 375 yards. Leo lost by a head, but the courageous horse was running on a bad knee.

No one knows for sure how many races Leo ran, but it has been reported that he won 20 of 22 starts. Nye also states that Bill Morgan of Pawhuska trained Leo during most of his racing career. Nye also stated the following about Leo:

"He is one of the fastest Quarter Horses ever brought into Osage County. He was the idol of track fans in and around Pawhuska, and was considered practically unbeatable while racing there, a belief well-founded as he lost but 2 of his 22 starts."

During his travels and changing ownerships, Leo was bred to several mares. One of the first was Swamp Angel, by Grano de Oro and out of the legendary Della

Leola, a 1948 AAA and AQHA Champion daughter of Leo. She was bred by Bud Warren, and was owned by Ed Honnen of Denver when this picture was taken.

Photo by Stewart's

Moore. While she was in foal to Leo, Swamp Angel was purchased in 1944 by Bud Warren, who was building a band of broodmares. Warren's breeding program in Perry, Okla., ultimately became extremely successful, putting him high on the list of leading breeders of Quarter running horses. And he became AQHA's 15th president in 1965.

In the mid-1940s, however, Warren was buying his first registered mares. Swamp Angel produced a filly, subsequently named Leota W, who became an outstanding racing filly, rated AAA. In fact, she was the 1947 Co-Champion Quarter Running 2-Year-Old.

Her prowess on the tracks, along with that of other Leo offspring such as Flit, AA, impressed Warren, and he decided he wanted to buy Leo for his breeding program. This he did in 1947, and Leo finally had a permanent home. It also marked the beginning of Leo's climb to legendary status as a sire, and Bud Warren's fame as a breeder.

Once he was settled in at Warren's ranch, Leo began attracting more mares who were better bred than some of the first mares to whom he was bred. He soon proved to be a prolific sire, and his offspring began burning up the tracks. But then, he incurred another serious injury in 1952 while breeding a mare. Warren had no choice but to stop breeding Leo for the remainder of that breeding season.

Reba Warren, Bud's widow, remembers

Another picture of Leola with her Three Bars (TB) colt, circa 1950s. According to Ed Honnen, the colt was stolen out of pasture at Ed's farm in Denver, and was never found. The colt was old enough to be weaned when he was taken.

Photo Courtesy of Phil Livingston

Sweet Leilani W, a Leo daughter foaled in 1951, who was AA and an AQHA Champion. She was bred by Bud Warren, but owned by Lou Tuck, Littleton, Colo., when this picture was taken in 1956 at the Laramie (Wyo.) Quarter Horse show, where she was the grand champion mare.

Photo by James Cathey

Robin Reed, a 1949 son of Leo who was AAAT and a sire of many ROM race colts. He was bred and owned by William Welch of St. Louis, Mo., and Granby, Colorado. **Photo by Doreen M. Norton, Courtesy of Phil Livingston**

She Kitty, a 1959 daughter of Robin Reed—and a Leo granddaughter—was a full sister to Old Tom Cat. She was AAAT and an AQHA Champion, and 1961 Champion Quarter Running 2-Year-Old. She was bred and owned by Jack Casement, Padroni, Colorado. **Photo by Ralph Morgan**

that Bud bought Leo Tag to finish the breeding season. Bud thought that Leo Tag, AAA, was one of Leo's best sons. Leo Tag was bred by A.E. Harper of Edmond, Okla., but Bud bought him from R.W. Patterson of Emmett, Idaho.

The fact that Leo was out of commission didn't stop his offspring from continuing to excel. Miss Meyers, Robin Reed, Oleo, and Leo Tag added to the reputation of their sire. Then came My Leo and Bobbie Leo, Leo Bob, Beauty Joleta, and Palleo Pete.

By 1955, when Leo was 15, his sons and daughters were becoming noted sires and producers through such individuals as Vanetta Dee, Vandy's Flash, and Goetta. He was also the great-grandsire of Tiny's Gay, who was out of Gay's Delight, who was out of Miss Ginger Gay by Palleo Pete.

Leo put lightning speed into many of his offspring, but his influence extended beyond the racetrack. His sons and daughters also showed up in halter and cutting competitions. It didn't take long for him to become recognized as a leading sire of arena horses.

Leo is best remembered as a broodmare sire, however. Space does not permit listing all of his daughters who became outstanding producers, but among the very best was Garrett's Miss Pawhuska, bred by Bill Rowe, Carlsbad, New Mexico. She was foaled in 1946 and was out of a Jimmie Allred mare named Jenny Dee. When bred to Vandy, Miss Pawhuska produced the likes of Vandy's Flash, Vanetta Dee, and Vannevar, all AAAT. Vandy's Flash was also the World Champion Quarter Running Gelding in 1958 and 1960, and World Champion Quarter Running Horse in 1960.

Vanetta Dee was the World Champion Quarter Running Mare in 1956, '57, and '58. And Vannevar was World Champion Quarter Running Gelding in 1956 and '57.

Miss Pawhuska also produced Vandy's Betty, Vansarita Too, and Miss Vanity, all AAA. Breeding this great mare to Vandy was a sure-fire ticket to getting a winner. Incidentally, she was often referred to as Miss Pawhuska, but she was registered as Garrett's Miss Pawhuska. Her owner was Dee Garrett of Pawhuska, Oklahoma.

Another great Leo daughter was South Pacific, a veritable equine factory. Foaled in 1954, she was out of the mare Randle's Lady, by Doc Horn (TB). In her lifetime, she produced 19 foals, of whom 10 earned

OLD TOM CAT

One of Robin Reed's best sons—and a Leo grandson—was Old Tom Cat, AAA and AQHA Champion. He was out of Little Meow, by Tadpole, was foaled in 1958, and bred and owned by Jack Casement, Padroni, Colorado.

ROMs in racing. Three foals were AA, four were AAA, and three were AAAT— Pacific Bars and Gofar Bar, both by Sugar Bars, and Pacific Jet, by Jet Deck.

Then there was Etta Leo, foaled in 1955 and out of the mare Bandette by Band Play. She produced 13 foals, including 3 who were AA, 4 who were AAA, and 3 who were AAAT. The latter included Goetta and Goetta 2, both by Go Man Go, and Ettabo, by Deep Sun (TB).

And still another Leo daughter was Flit, who was foaled in 1945 and was out of a Triangle mare. She produced 17 foals, including 2 who were AAA, and several who earned their fame in the arena, such as King's Pistol and Sugar Leo, both AQHA Champions. King's Pistol was also the 1957 NCHA World Champion Cutting Horse. Flit's offspring included 7 who earned 152 AQHA halter points, while 5 earned 77.5 performance points.

Another of Bud Warren's favorite Leo sons was Croton Oil, a full brother to South Pacific. In the April 1966 issue of *The Quarter Horse Journal*, Garford Wilkinson quoted Warren as saying:

Flit, a 1945 daughter of Leo, was AA. She went on to produce 17 foals.
Photo Courtesy of Reba Warren

Rosa Leo, a 1953 AAA Leo daughter in the winner's circle at Bay Meadows (California), on January 12, 1957. Owned by Bud Warren, she was trained by C.M. Kiser and ridden by L. Littell.

Photo Courtesy of Reba Warren

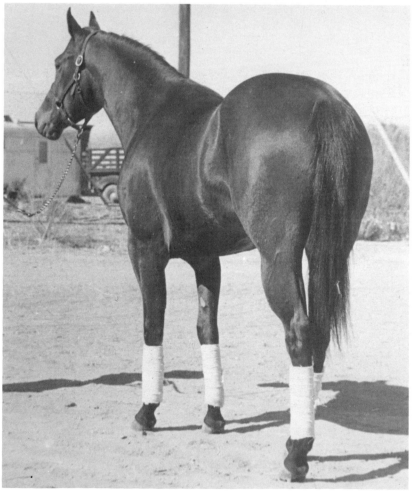

Leota W, one of Leo's first daughters who started him on the road to fame as a sire. She was AAA.

"Croton Oil is my personal favorite, possibly because he carries the stamp and style of Leo more than any other horse I've ever known."

Croton Oil sired 13 AQHA Champions and 62 foals who earned ROMs in racing— including Miss Croton Oil and Croton's Jill, both AAAT.

Leo San was another outstanding son. Out of San Sue Darks, by San Siemon, he was foaled in 1949. In addition to Peppy San and Mr San Peppy, he also sired Wimpy Leo San, 1961 high-point halter horse; and Leo San Van, 1961 high-point halter *and* cutting gelding, 1962 high-point cutting gelding, and an AQHA Champion.

Leo also sired one Supreme Champion, Leo Maudie, who was also AAA. He was foaled in 1961, and was out of Maudie Williams, by Billy Anson.

However, Leo daughters produced seven Supreme Champions:

Sugar Rocket, by Rocket Bar (TB) and out of Sugar Mayday.

Jet Threat, AAA, by Jet Deck and out of Rosita Leo.

Coldstream Guard, AAA, by Afton Creek (TB) and out of Miss Adelita.

Goodbye Sam, AAA, by Fairfax Joe and out of Maudie Leo.

Milk River, AAA, by Custus Rastus (TB) and out of Leolib.

Kid Meyers, AAA, by Three Bars (TB) and out of Miss Meyers.

And, finally, Fairbars, AAA, by Three

George Tyler showing Leo San Siemon—by Leo San, by Leo—at the 1962 Houston Livestock Show, where he was grand champion stallion. He was owned by Rebecca Tyler of Gainesville, Texas.

Bars (TB) and out of Lady Fairfax.

While many of Leo's get compiled outstanding racing and arena records, a sizable number of his colts became geldings who excelled under saddle, but achieved no particular fame, or AQHA record.

Bud Warren passed away January 15, 1988, at the age of 77. About a year before his death, however, he talked with this writer (Diane Simmons) about Leo:

"I guess a lot of people thought I was crazy when I bought a crippled stallion, but somehow I knew that that horse would be a sire.

"He was always a pleasure to be around, and I don't think any of us will ever realize what he contributed to this industry. He left his mark everywhere. He stamped his offspring in looks and disposition. He put heart and try into them and, just like their daddy, most of them didn't know when to say quit. That was Leo.

"By the time he was 23, his old knee injury was causing a lot of trouble. It was getting bigger and bigger. We did everything we could, but we couldn't seem to slow down the calcium buildup.

"It reached a point that it was so bad,

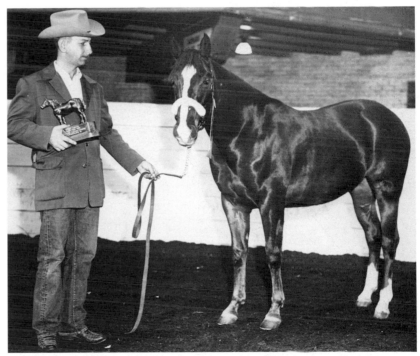

Bud Warren and Leolita, a AAA AQHA Champion daughter of Leo and Swamp Angel, foaled in 1959. This picture was taken at the Chicago International Livestock Show where she was reserve grand champion mare. Circa 1950s. **Equestrian Illustrative Photo**

South Pacific, another terrific Leo daughter, produced 19 foals after she was retired from the track. This photo was taken at Enid, Okla., in July 1957. The mare had just won a 350-yarder in 19.3. That's Bud Warren on the left.

Photo Courtesy of Reba Warren

Leo Tag, a 1949 AAA AQHA son of Leo and Tagalong. After Bud Warren used him for breeding and racing, he eventually was owned by Dee Burk of Wagoner, Oklahoma.

Leo San Van, a Leo grandson who earned Superiors in both halter and cutting. He was AQHA's high-point cutting gelding in 1961 and 1962, and high-point halter gelding in 1961. He was owned by the Howell Quarter Horse Ranch, Seagoville, Tex., and shown by Matlock Rose.

Garrett's Miss Pawhuska was rated only A on the track, but produced a number of speed burners when she was bred to Vandy. This picture was taken at the 1948 Oklahoma 2-Year-Old Futurity. She was owned by Dee Garrett and piloted by Bobby Mitchell.

Photo Courtesy of Reba Warren

he'd get down and couldn't get up. We'd go out to the barn and help him, put bales of hay around him, anything we could do to help him get a little relief. He'd be on his feet a few days and then go down again. He was healthy in every other way, but the constant struggle with that knee literally wore him out.

"Then the day came when he got down and couldn't get up, even with our help. He tried as hard as he could. He knew he wasn't sick. He knew he didn't feel bad other than the pain of that knee. He struggled and struggled but it just wouldn't support him. He gave it everything he had.

"He tried so hard he was hurting himself. He kept hitting against the stall, bumping his head, bruising himself. We decided the only remaining kindness we could give him was to put him to sleep.

"He's resting on that hill across from the house, with a tombstone. Leo was about as good as they'll ever come."

Leo died in 1967. He was 27.

A 1964 picture of Bud Warren with Croton Oil, one of Warren's favorite Leo sons. **Photo by Pat Close**

PROFILE

DIANE SIMMONS began her career in journalism with the Scripps-Howard newspaper chain, while still working on her degree at Memphis State University. She relocated to southern California after graduating in 1970.

Diane grew up in an agricultural area outside Memphis, and spent many hours pleasure riding. She left the horses behind when she moved to Los Angeles, but found them again in 1975 when she decided to begin free-lance writing, with a major emphasis on horses.

She sold her first free-lance article to an East Coast equine publication. The subject of the article, rodeo horses, intrigued the magazine's predominantly eastern readers. Less than 2 months later, Diane became involved with the controversy concerning several bands of wild horses in the Challis, Ida., area. Working in conjunction with the Bureau of Land Management, she ended up with the only set of photographs of the band that was soon to become the wild horse test case in Washington, D.C. Her stories, behavioral studies, and pictures relating to the roaming bands were seen in several major equine publications over the next year.

By 1980, Diane's horse-related work was being carried in 12 publications, including *Western Horseman, American Horseman, Horse of Course, Horse & Rider, California Horse Review, Paint Horse Journal, Rodeo News, Horse Illustrated*, and *Speedhorse*. She was one of

Diane Simmons and her Cocker Spaniel.

the first equine journalists to begin working directly with veterinarians, providing medical/health articles in layman's terminology for a number of magazines. Her work even extended into publications such as *Art West* with assignments on equine and/or western artists.

Although Diane worked with all forms of show, performance, and halter, she gravitated toward the racing segment of the horse industry and, since 1978, that has been her primary area of concentration. Now living in north Texas, she has served as editor for *Speedhorse/The Racing Report* since 1984. Her race-related editorials have received the American Quarter Horse Association Sprint Award twice, and her work was also reviewed in *The Best American Sports Writing of 1991*.

REFERENCES

The following books and magazines were among those used for reference for this book:

That Special Breed, The American Quarter Horse, by Lyn Jank. Published in 1977 by Branch-Smith Inc., 120 St. Louis Ave., Fort Worth, TX 76104; 817-877-1314.

Outstanding Modern Quarter Horse Sires, by Nelson C. Nye. Published in 1948 by William Morrow & Company, New York City. (Out of print.)

The Great American Speedhorse, A Guide to Quarter Racing, by Walt Wiggins. Copyrighted in 1978 by Walt Wiggins. Published by Sovereign Books, a Simon & Schuster Division of Gulf & Western Corporation, New York City. (Out of print.)

The King Ranch Quarter Horses, by Robert Moorman Denhardt. Published in 1970 by the University of Oklahoma Press, 1005 Asp Ave., Norman, OK 73019; 1-800-627-7377 or 405-325-5111.

They Rode Good Horses, The First Fifty Years of the American Quarter Horse Association, by Don Hedgpeth. Published in 1990 by the American Quarter Horse Association, Box 200, Amarillo, TX 79104; 806-376-4811.

Speed and the Quarter Horse—A Payload of Sprinters, by Nelson C. Nye. Copyrighted in 1973 by Nelson C. Nye. Published by The Caxton Printers Ltd., Caldwell, ID 83605; sold through Premier Publishing, Box 137, Wamego, KS 66547; 913-456-2074.

The Quarter Running Horse, America's Oldest Breed, by Robert Moorman Denhardt. Published in 1979 by the University of Oklahoma Press, 1005 Asp Ave., Norman, OK 73019; 1-800-627-7377 or 405-325-5111.

The Quarter Running Horse 1947 and 1948 Year Books, published by the American Quarter Racing Association, Tucson, Arizona. (Out of print.)

The Quarter Horse, published by the National Quarter Horse Breeders Association, Knox City, Texas. (Out of print.)

The Most Influential Quarter Horse Sires, by Andrea Laycock Pitzer. Copyrighted in 1987 by Andrea Laycock Pitzer. Published by Premier Pedigrees, Puyallup, Wash.; sold through Premier Publishing, Box 137, Wamego, KS 66547; 913-456-2074.

Quarter Horse Reference, Volume I, by Don M. Wagoner. Published in 1972 by Quarter Horse Reference, Box 487, Grapevine, TX 76051. (We believe it is out of print.)

Great Horses of the Past, Volume I, by Bob Gray. Published in 1967 by Cordovan Corporation, Houston. (Out of print.)

Champions of the Quarter Track, by Nelson C. Nye. Published in 1950 by Coward-McCann Inc., New York City. (Out of print.)

Great Moments in Quarter Racing History, by Nelson C. Nye. Published in 1983 by Arco Publishing Inc., New York City. (Out of print.)

Speedhorse Magazine, Box 1000, Norman, OK 73070.

The Quarter Horse Journal, Box 32470, Amarillo, TX 79120.

Western Horseman Magazine

Colorado Springs, Colorado

The Western Horseman Magazine, established in 1936, is the world's leading horse publication. For subscription information and a list of other Western Horseman books, contact: Western Horseman Magazine, Box 7980, Colorado Springs, CO 80933-7980; 719-633-5524.